Legal Rights of Hearing-Impaired People

Authors

Sy DuBow
Legal Director
National Center for Law and the Deaf
(NCLD)
J.D., George Washington University

Larry Goldberg
Associate Legal Director, NCLD
J.D., George Washington University

Sarah Geer
Staff Attorney
National Association of the Deaf
Legal Defense Fund
Staff Attorney, NCLD, 1978–81
J.D., University of North Carolina

Elaine Gardner
Staff Attorney, NCLD
J.D., Georgetown University

Andrew Penn
Attorney
Goldfarb, Singer, and Austern
Staff Attorney, NCLD, 1978–81
J.D., University of California, Berkeley

Sheila Conlon
Staff Attorney, NCLD
J.D., Georgetown University

Marc Charmatz
Litigation Attorney
National Association of the Deaf
Legal Defense Fund
J.D., Northwestern University

LEGAL RIGHTS
of Hearing-Impaired People

National Center for Law
and the Deaf

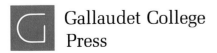
Gallaudet College
Press

Second Edition 1984
Published by Gallaudet College Press
Washington, DC 20002

Library of Congress Cataloging in Publication Data
Legal rights of hearing-impaired people.

   Authors, Sy DuBow, and others.
   Includes index.
   1. Deaf—Legal status, laws, etc.—United States.
I. DuBow, Sy. II. National Center for Law and the Deaf (U.S.)
KF480.5.D4L43 1982b   346.7301'3   83-20710
ISBN 0-913580-90-2   347.30613

The National Center for Law and the Deaf is a public service of Gallaudet
College, 800 Florida Avenue NE, Washington, DC 20002, telephone (202)
651-5454 (Voice/TDD).

Gallaudet College is an equal opportunity employer/educational institution.
Programs and services offered by Gallaudet College receive substantial
financial support from the U.S. Department of Education.

In memory of Fred Schreiber, the happy warrior for deaf people's rights

Contents

Preface

Hearing-impaired people are confronted with barriers to communication throughout and in all aspects of their lives.

Recent state and federal laws have begun to break down these barriers. This book explains how these laws can help hearing-impaired people in areas where their needs have been ignored or inadequately addressed.

We have tried to provide one comprehensive and current resource on legal rights and remedies for hearing-impaired citizens. We also describe flexible ways to ensure effective communication and better understanding through technological advances, interpreting alternatives, and deaf awareness.

In the 1980s there have been threats to cut back on legal protections for disabled people. But organizations of and for disabled people have caused the federal government to withdraw attempts to weaken regulations under the Education for All Handicapped Children Act and Section 504 of the Rehabilitation Act of 1973. There has also been a positive trend in court decisions, especially at the federal appellate level, to evaluate individual ability on a factual record. With increasing frequency, courts are striking down exclusionary policies grounded on stereotypic attitudes and unsupported fears.

Our democratic society has a responsibility to ensure that all its citizens, including those with disabilities, are given an equal opportunity to lead productive lives. This book discusses the legal tools now available to all citizens concerned with securing this fundamental equality.

NATIONAL CENTER FOR
  LAW AND THE DEAF
GALLAUDET COLLEGE
WASHINGTON, DC 20002

NOVEMBER 21, 1983

SY DUBOW

Acknowledgments

The authors offer special thanks to Jim Johnson, former Projects Editor at the National Center for Law and the Deaf (NCLD), for his initial editing of this book.

Permission to use copyrighted material was kindly granted by

Houghton Mifflin Company, for a quotation in Chapter Three;

Legal Services Corporation, for parts of Chapters Three, Four, Five, Seven, and Nine;

Grune & Stratton Incorporated, for the substance of Chapter Six;

The Deaf American, for a section of Chapter Twelve;

University of Richmond Law Review, for Appendix B.

Cover and text illustrations are by Laura Warren Stutzman. The staff of Gallaudet College's Art and Photography Services produced many of the photographs. Other photographs were provided courtesy of the

National Technical Institute for the Deaf (pages 22, 45, 76, 80, 90, 103, 113, 140);

National Captioning Institute, Inc. (pages 21, 135);

Washington Post (page 153);

U.S. Geological Survey (page 143);

International Association of Chiefs of Police (page 122).

Parts of several chapters originally appeared in NCLD newsletters and special reports and were adapted for inclusion here.

CHAPTER ONE
Communicating with Hearing-Impaired People

More than merely a barrier to sound perception, hearing loss is a barrier to communication and understanding. It is a major, chronic disability that affects one out of every sixteen Americans. One in every 100 Americans is profoundly deaf— unable to hear speech well enough to understand it.[1] The wide range of impairment, the variety of methods of communication, and differences in the age of onset of disability make it difficult to generalize about deaf people. But certain facts are apparent.

Deaf people rely on information they can see. Some means of making communication visible is necessary to ensure that deaf people are able to explain their needs effectively and understand what is expected of them. With some auxiliary aid or accommodation and some sensitivity to their condition by those around, deaf people can communicate and participate fully and easily in most settings.

Deaf people have not received fair treatment from professional, social, and government service providers or from the courts and police. Some accommodation to the condition of deafness can make a critical difference in whether deaf people receive services they need and to which they are entitled and whether they can participate satisfactorily in society. The material cost of such accommodation is modest in comparison with the gain realized.

As we review the various methods that deaf people use to communicate, one general rule to bear in mind is that the deaf person knows what method is best, because he or she has spent a lifetime negotiating the problems that deafness imposes. Whatever method is natural for that person is the method that should always be used, preferably from the first moment of contact.

Sign Language and Interpreters

American Sign Language (ASL) is a visible language that is linguistically independent of English. Its signals are handshapes and movements that represent words, concepts, or letters of the English alphabet. Many deaf people use sign language rather than English as their primary mode of communication. For many deaf people it is a native language with rich cultural associations.

An interpreter is a skilled professional who can translate the meaning of spoken words into sign language as the words are spoken and translate sign language messages into correct English as they are signed. Interpretation of written or spoken English into ASL requires a high degree of skill. It takes as much time and effort to learn sign language as any other language.

At times a specialized interpreter must be used. For example, a person who is both deaf and visually impaired may need a specially trained deaf-blind interpreter. Some deaf people do not use sign language but require an "oral" interpreter who silently mouths the speaker's words to them. The oral interpreter is usually a person whom the deaf person finds easy to lipread and who knows how to substitute synonyms for words that are difficult to lipread. Another unusual situation occurs when the deaf person has rudimentary language skills or does not use conventional sign language. In this situation, another deaf person may have to provide interpretation into conventional sign language, which can then be interpreted into English by the regular interpreter.

Qualified interpreters can be found through local and state chapters of the Registry of Interpreters for the Deaf (RID), a national professional organization that certifies interpreters in various skill specialties, including legal interpreting.[2] Interpreters can also be located through local organizations of deaf people, the state association of the deaf, a state commission or agency for hearing-impaired people, or schools for deaf children. In addition, deaf people may themselves suggest local interpreters. Professional offices and service agencies should develop their own lists of interpreters whom they know to be reliable and competent.

Using the same interpreter regularly can enhance the quality of the communication, since an interpreter who is familiar with a speaker's vocal style and customary phrases will be able to interpret more effectively. The interpreter also can provide valuable assistance to service providers by advising them about effective use of an interpreter and about other means of communicating with deaf people.

While professional certification may be useful in evaluating the skills of an interpreter, the ultimate authority on an interpreter's qualifications should be the deaf person. An interpreter who cannot provide effective communication to a deaf person in a particular situation cannot be considered qualified despite professional certification.

Relying on amateurs who may know some sign language is a frequent error.

Interpreter Guidelines

A professional interpreter should uphold the National Registry of Interpreters for the Deaf Code of Ethics, which carefully defines the role of an interpreter. This code prohibits an interpreter from continuing in any assignment if attempts to communicate are unsuccessful for either party.

The following are guidelines for use of interpreters:

- When talking, look at the deaf person, not the interpreter; speak directly to the person as if the interpreter were not present. For example, say, "The hearing will be on Tuesday," rather than, "Tell him that the hearing will be on Tuesday." The interpreter will sign exactly what is said.

- Some deaf people will speak for themselves. Others will not speak, so the interpreter will say in English what the person signs. In both cases, respond by talking to the deaf person, not the interpreter.

- The interpreter should be directly beside the speaker so that he or she is easily visible to the deaf person.

- The interpreter should not be placed in shadows or in front of any source of bright light, such as a window.

- No private conversation should occur with the interpreter or with anyone else in the deaf person's presence. The interpreter must interpret everything that is said in front of the deaf person. Any discussion of the deaf person's language or communication level should take place privately with the interpreter. Ask the deaf person, not the interpreter, if he or she understands what is being said.

- Speak naturally and not too fast. Remember that names and some other words must be fingerspelled and that this takes more time than signing. The interpreter will indicate whether it is necessary to slow down. Avoid jargon or other technical words with which the deaf person may be unfamiliar. If possible, meet with the interpreter before the interview to discuss the best way to interpret certain technical concepts into sign language without losing any of the meaning.

- Make sure that the interpreter understands the need for complete confidentiality. Do not allow the interpreter to discuss the deaf person's problems with the person or to give any advice about the problem. The interpreter's only role is to facilitate communication with the deaf person.

The ability to make or read a few signs or to fingerspell is no substitute for proficiency. A well-meaning, beginning signer will usually not know sign language well enough to interpret or to communicate effectively with most deaf people.

Many inexperienced interpreters do not sign in ASL but use signs borrowed from ASL in an English word order. They may frequently impose a completely incorrect English meaning on a sign, such as using the sign for the adjective *fine*, meaning "good," to connote the noun *fine*, meaning "penalty." An unqualified interpreter might fingerspell words when he or she does not know a sign; but directly translated English idioms are rendered meaningless in ASL. For example, a direct translation of the English idiom *have to* would mean "possess" in ASL.

Problems of Notewriting

Many deaf people rely on written notes to communicate with hearing people or to supplement other modes of communication. However, writing is not always effective or appropriate. A written conversation is tedious, cumbersome, and time-consuming. Written messages are frequently condensed. The writer omits much of the information that would otherwise be exchanged, so the deaf person does not get the same amount of detail that a hearing person would.

Some deaf people are highly educated. Others are not. A common

misconception is that deaf people compensate for their inability to hear by reading and writing. Many deaf people, especially those who lost their hearing before they learned to talk, have difficulty with written as well as spoken English. Data from a 1971 national survey of hearing-impaired students showed that reading comprehension is the hearing-impaired person's most difficult academic area. It is the area most severely affected by deafness.[3]

Most people learn their native language by hearing it spoken around them from infancy. But a person who is born deaf or who loses the ability to hear when very young cannot learn English in this way. Therefore, despite normal intelligence, a deaf person may have limited competence in English. For such people, English is virtually a second language. They may have a limited English vocabulary and grammar, a condition that can lead to numerous misunderstandings.

The extensive use of idioms in English also poses significant reading problems for deaf people. For example, the expression *under arrest* in the *Miranda* warnings (discussed in Chapter Nine) would be puzzling to many deaf people because *under* to them means only "beneath."[4] For these reasons, written notes or materials will often be inadequate to achieve effective communication with a deaf person. The effectiveness of notewriting as a method should be observed carefully to avoid miscommunication.

Lipreading Comprehension

A common misconception about deaf people is that they all read lips. Very few people can read lips well enough to understand speech, even under optimum conditions. Information collected during the 1972 National Census of the Deaf Population indicated that 21.4 percent of deaf adults who completed one or more years of senior high school considered their lipreading ability to be poor to nonexistent.[5] "In fact, even the best speechreaders in a one-to-one situation were found to understand only 26 percent of what was said [and m]any bright deaf individuals grasp less than 5 percent."[6]

This low level of comprehension occurs because many English speech sounds are not visible on the mouth or lips. Certain spoken words or sounds create similar lip movements. The ambiguity of lipreading is demonstrated by the fact that the sounds of T, D, Z, S, and N all look identical on the lips. The words *right, ride,* and *rise* would be indistinguishable to a deaf person, as would the sentences, "Do you have the time?" and "Do you have the dime?" The meaning of entire sentences can be lost because a key word is missed or misunderstood. When a deaf person does not understand a sentence, the speaker should repeat the thought using different words. The speaker should use gestures freely, for example, pointing to a wristwatch to indicate time.

Many factors hinder one's ability to lipread. Lipreading is difficult when

- the speaker is in motion or not directly facing the lipreader;
- the lips are obscured by hands, beards, or mustaches;
- the speaker does not articulate carefully or has distorted speech;
- the speaker has a regional or foreign accent;
- the speaker is using technical or unfamiliar words;
- the lipreader is not familiar with the language structures and vocabulary of spoken English;
- the speaker is not well-lighted;
- the lipreader must look into a glare or light;
- the lipreader has poor vision.

Lipreading often supplements other modes of communication, but it is seldom sufficient in itself to ensure effective communication. Unless the deaf person indicates a preference for using only lipreading, it should not be relied upon extensively.

Environmental Interferences

Environmental factors often interfere with communication with a deaf person. The room should be adequately lighted, without glare. While profoundly deaf people will not be affected by background noises, they will be distracted by a great deal of background movement or changes in lighting. A person who uses a hearing aid or who has residual hearing may be seriously distracted by background noises. One should try to talk in a quiet place, away from the noises of machinery and other conversations.

When talking to a hearing-impaired person, one should speak directly to the person without moving around, turning away, or looking down at papers or books. Speak naturally, without shouting or distorting normal mouth movements.

Some deaf people have normal and intelligible speech. Others do not speak

at all. Early deafness interferes with language and speech acquisition. Many deaf people who can speak exhibit unusual tones, inflections, or modulations. Whether or not a deaf person uses speech is a matter of individual preference. Difficulty in understanding a deaf person's voice can be relieved by listening without interruption for a while until the person's particular voice patterns become familiar.

The phrases "deaf-mute" and "deaf and dumb" are considered by most deaf people to be insults and should not be used.

Communication Devices

One frustration of deafness is the inability to use a conventional telephone. Hearing people rely heavily on the tele-phone and take it for granted in communicating with businesses, friends, government agencies, and emergency services. With new devices for deaf people coming into more frequent use, the telephone has become a means rather than a barrier to communication.

A TDD (Telecommunication Device for the Deaf), commonly referred to as a TTY (teletypewriter), is a machine with a typewriter keyboard connected by an acoustic coupler to a regular tele-phone.* Two people with compatible equipment can have a typed conversation over the telephone, enabling hear-ing- and speech-impaired people to have the same functional telephone service as other people. The devices are relatively inexpensive and easy to use.

If a professional, agency, or business office does not have a TDD, deaf people will not be able to get information, make appointments, or transact business by telephone. The office will be unable to contact deaf clients except by mail, resulting in frustrating delays, inefficient service, and lost business. The office should publicize the fact that its telephone is TDD-equipped and should

---

*Although most deaf people use the term TTY generically to refer to any of several telecommunications devices, technically TTY refers only to converted teletypewriter machines. The broader term TDD includes not only the TTY but also new video and electronic machines such as the C-Phone, Manual Communications Module (MCM), and Portatel. Hereafter we will regularly use the inclusive term TDD; in certain contexts, however, the more common, everyday term TTY will be used.

indicate this fact in all telephone directory listings and on all announcements, brochures, and letterheads. The TDD capability is indicated by placing the letters "(TDD)" after the phone number or by "(Voice or TDD)" if both options are available.

Other devices are available which adapt telephones to the individual needs of hearing-impaired people. Amplifier switches can be added to telephone receivers. Telephones and other auditory systems—alarms, doorbells, or inhome buzzers—can be connected to a blinking light which alerts a hearing-impaired person. Many hearing aids are equipped with inductive coil "telephone switches." These hearing aids use electromagnetic leakage from compatible telephone receivers to transmit the message. If, in a job situation, a person using this kind of hearing aid is assigned to an incompatible telephone, a compatible model can be acquired at reasonable cost.

The methods described above are those most commonly used by hearing-impaired people. They are the means of crossing and thus eliminating the communications barriers that separate deaf and hearing people from one another.

Notes

1. J. Schein and M. Delk, *The Deaf Population of the United States* (Silver Spring, Md.: National Association of the Deaf, 1974), p. 15.

2. The national office of the Registry of Interpreters for the Deaf is located at 814 Thayer Avenue, Silver Spring, MD 20910. Telephone (301) 588-2406.

3. Gallaudet College, *Academic Achievement Test Results of a National Testing Program for Hearing-Impaired Students in the United States*, Spring 1971 monograph.

4. Mary Furey, personal communication, June 1976.

5. Schein and Delk, *Deaf Population*, p. 63.

6. M. Vernon and E. Mindel, *They Grow in Silence: The Deaf Child and His Family* (Silver Spring, Md.: National Association of the Deaf, 1971), p. 96.

CHAPTER TWO
The Rehabilitation Act of 1973

Historically, disabled people have been unemployed and underemployed. In 1920 Congress passed the first federal laws to help disabled people get job training and find employment. But these laws were clearly inadequate; even qualified disabled people could not find good jobs because of widespread discrimination against them by private employers and by federal, state, and local governments. Congress addressed the problem by enacting the Rehabilitation Act of 1973, Title V of which has been hailed as a "bill of rights" for disabled people.

The purpose of Title V is to make sure that programs receiving federal money can be used by all disabled people. The four major sections of Title V prohibit discrimination and require accessibility in employment, education, and health, welfare, and social services.

Section 501 applies to federal government employment practices.[1] It requires of each executive department and agency, including the U.S. Postal Service, an affirmative action plan for the hiring, placement, and advancement of qualified handicapped people. (For more information, see Chapter Seven, Employment.)

Section 502 creates the Architectural and Transportation Barriers Compliance Board.[2] The board's primary functions are to ensure compliance with a 1968 federal law prohibiting architectural barriers in federally funded buildings and to eliminate barriers from public transportation systems. (For more information, see Chapter Eight, Architectural Barriers.)

Section 503 requires affirmative action in the hiring, placement, and promotion of qualified handicapped people by employers who have contracts or subcontracts with the federal government of more than $2,500 a year.[3] Contractors with fifty or more employees or contracts for more than $50,000 are also required to have written affirmative action plans. (See Chapter Seven, Employment.)

Section 504 prohibits discrimination against qualified handicapped people in any federally supported program or activity.[4] Recipients of federal financial assistance include most public and some private institutions, from schools and nursing homes to museums and airports. This chapter will be devoted to the implementation, regulation, and application of Section 504.

Section 504

As amended in 1978, Section 504 of the Rehabilitation Act reads:

> No otherwise qualified handicapped individual in the United States . . . shall, solely by reason of his handicap, be excluded from participation in, be denied the benefits of, or be subjected to discrimination under any program or activity receiving federal financial assistance or under any program or activity conducted by any Executive Agency or by the United States Postal Service.[5]

The statute is implemented by detailed regulations that every federal agency giving financial assistance must promulgate, spelling out the Section 504 obligations of its recipients.[6] In 1977 the U.S. Department of Health, Education, and Welfare (HEW)* became the first agency to publish its

---

*HEW was divided into two cabinet-level departments—the Departments of Education (ED) and of Health and Human Services (HHS)—effective May 4, 1980. Hereafter, references to HEW will be restricted to actions taken before that date. Unless noted otherwise, HEW policies remain in effect at ED and HHS.

regulation and detailed analysis.[7] The department also issued a set of standards for other agencies to use in developing their own Section 504 regulations. Primary authority to monitor the regulations of the agencies was given to the Department of Justice in 1980.

Who Must Obey Section 504

The federal government assists many programs and activities around the country. The HHS regulation defines "federal financial assistance" as "any grant, loan, contract (other than a procurement contract or a contract of insurance or guaranty), or any other arrangement by which the Department provides or otherwise makes available assistance in the form of funds or services of federal personnel or property."[8] The exclusion of procurement contracts means that private businesses that manufacture items purchased by the government do not have to obey

Section 504. However, they are subject to Section 503, which prohibits employment discrimination. Some organizations have both procurement contracts with and financial assistance from the federal government. They have to obey both Sections 503 and 504 of the law.

Because the definition of federal financial assistance is so broad, many private as well as public institutions must obey Section 504. The types of institutions usually receiving some form of federal financial assistance include elementary and secondary schools, colleges and universities, hospitals, nursing homes, vocational rehabilitation agencies, public welfare offices, state and local governments, police and fire departments, correction and probation departments, libraries, museums, theater programs, parks, recreational facilities, mass transit systems, airports and harbors, subsidized housing programs, legal services programs, and most parts of the judicial system.

Section 504 is applicable whether the federal assistance is received directly or indirectly, for example, through a state or local government. A "recipient" is defined as any institution that receives federal assistance or that indirectly benefits from such assistance.

Sometimes it is difficult to determine

whether and from what agency an institution gets federal financial assistance. If the institution is public, citizens usually can examine its financial records and reports to see if it receives federal assistance. Many federal agencies keep public lists of the programs and activities they fund. If the agency does not have such a list, or if the particular institution is not listed, a request can be filed under the Freedon of Information Act (FOIA) with each federal agency thought to be the funding source.[9]

The FOIA request should identify the possible recipient, state that the information is being sought under the Freedom of Information Act, and ask if the particular institution receives federal financial assistance and, if so, for what purpose. It is important to identify the institution fully and correctly and to give the name and address of any parent organization(s) to which it belongs. For example, a local branch library may not be listed as a direct recipient of federal assistance. Instead, the state, regional, or county association may be the formal recipient. The federal agency is supposed to respond to an FOIA request within ten days.

A complaint against an institution for violation of Section 504 can be filed with a federal agency even if it is not clear whether that institution gets financial assistance from that agency. If the agency does not assist that institution, the agency will simply refuse to accept the complaint.

Obligations of Recipients

If an institution receives any federal financial assistance for one part of its activities, then it must obey Section 504 in all of its activities which "receive or benefit from" the financial assistance, even if those other activities do not receive any direct aid.[10]

For example, if the federal Law Enforcement Assistance Administration gives a local police department money for a new radio system, that police department must obey Section 504 in all of its activities, not just those affected by its radio system. If a deaf person is arrested, the police department would be obligated to provide a qualified interpreter immediately to advise that person of his or her rights. An exception to this general application is the proposed Office of Revenue Sharing (ORS) regulation which says that Section 504 applies only if the program or activity itself is funded "in whole or in part" with ORS funds.[11]

Since 1978, Section 504 has applied to federal executive agencies and the U.S. Postal Service as well as to recipients of federal financial assistance. Because the original 1973 law did not apply to federal agencies, the current Section 504 regulations are all written to apply only to recipients of assistance from the agency and not to the agency itself. Since the 1978 amendments, however, the agencies themselves must obey Section 504, whether or not they have adopted specific regulations that apply to their own activities.

Who is Protected by Section 504

Section 504 protects people with many different kinds of physical and mental disabilities. The definition of "handicapped" adopted by HEW is very broad. It includes any person who (1) has a physical or mental impairment that substantially limits one or more major life activity, (2) has a record of such an impairment, or (3) is regarded as having such an impairment.[12]

Major life activities are defined as "taking care of oneself," walking, hearing, doing manual tasks, seeing, speaking, breathing, learning, and working. Section 504 therefore protects almost anyone with a disabling condition, whether due to a congenital handicap, disease, accident, or any other reason.

For example, Section 504 protects deaf, hard-of-hearing, and blind people; people in wheelchairs; people with ce-rebral palsy, diabetes, epilepsy, cancer, speech defects, or emotional disturbance; former alcoholics or drug addicts; and mentally retarded people. A person who is not actually disabled but who is considered handicapped in some way is still protected by Section 504. For example, people who experienced mental illness in the past may encounter employers unwilling to hire them because of their history of illness. Such persons are protected by Section 504 even though they are not ill at the present time. The law also protects people who were misdiagnosed or misclassified as handicapped.

Section 504 does not guarantee handicapped people jobs or services merely because they are handicapped. To be protected by Section 504, a handicapped person must also be "qualified" for the job or service in question. The HEW regulation defines a "qualified handicapped person" as:

- With respect to employment, a handicapped person who with reasonable accommodation, can perform the essential functions of the job in question.
- With respect to public preschool, elementary, secondary, or adult education, a handicapped person (i) of an age during which nonhandicapped persons are provided such services, (ii) of any age during which it is mandatory under state law to provide such services to handicapped persons, or (iii) to whom a state is required to provide a free appropriate public education under §612 of the Education for All Handicapped Children Act; and

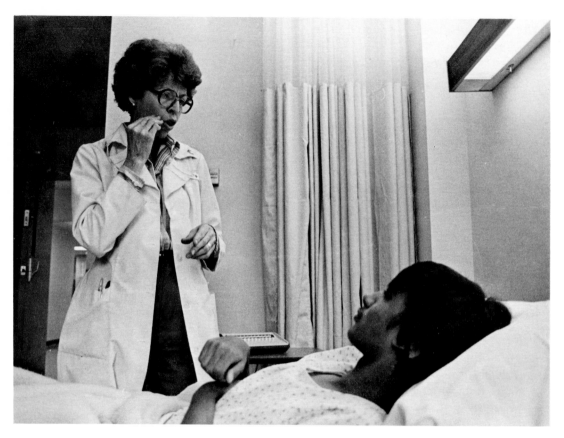

• With respect to postsecondary and vocational education services, a handicapped person who meets the academic and technical standards requisite to admission or participation in the recipient's education program or activity; and

• With respect to other services, a handicapped person who meets the essential eligibility requirements for the receipt of such services.[13]

A handicapped person must fall under the applicable definition in order to be protected by the nondiscrimination provisions of Section 504.

General Nondiscrimination Provisions

The HEW Section 504 regulation lists general categories of discriminatory behavior against handicapped people which are prohibited. It also establishes broad policy guidelines to determine whether a particular discriminatory act is prohibited by Section 504.

Equal opportunity. The most significant principle is that no recipient or federal agency may deny, on the basis of handicap, a qualified person an opportunity to participate in or benefit from its programs or services.[14] A federally funded program cannot refuse to serve a handicapped person merely because of that handicap. A deaf person cannot be denied admission to a mental health counseling program merely because he or she is deaf. If a counseling program is available only to people who live in a certain county, however, and the deaf person does not live in that county, he or she can be denied admission to the program for that particular reason.

A handicapped person must be given an opportunity to participate in or benefit from a program in a manner that is equal to and as effective as the opportunity provided to nonhandicapped people.[15] To be equally effective, a program does not have to produce the identical result or level of achievement for handicapped and nonhandicapped participants; the requirement is only that handicapped people be provided an equal opportunity to obtain the same result, to gain the same benefit, or to reach the same level of achievement as nonhandicapped people.[16] For example, the administrator of an adult education program might tell a deaf person simply to read the written materials for a class, without attending lectures and discussions. This would be unfair. Because the lectures and discussions help to explain and amplify the written material, the deaf person would not have an equal opportunity to benefit from the class.

Different or special treatment.
Sometimes handicapped people will need different or special treatment in order to give them genuine equal opportunity. In the area of race or sex discrimination, equal opportunity usually means treating people in exactly the same way. But a handicapped person may need some special assistance or accommodation in order to get benefits or services equivalent to a nonhandicapped person. Failure to provide that special assistance or accommodation would constitute discrimination. As explained in the analysis accompanying the HEW Section 504 regulation:

> [D]ifferent or special treatment of handicapped persons because of their handicaps, may be necessary in a number of contexts in order to assure equal opportunity. Thus, for example, it is meaningless to "admit" a handicapped person in a wheelchair to a program if the program is offered only on the third floor of a walk-up building. Nor is one providing equal educational opportunity to a deaf child by admitting him or her to a classroom but providing no means for the child to understand the teacher or receive instruction.[17]

At the same time, Section 504 also prohibits unnecessary special or different treatment if it would tend to stigmatize handicapped people or set them apart from nonhandicapped people. Different or separate aids, benefits, or services to handicapped people are prohibited unless the separation is necessary to provide them with services that are as effective as those provided to others.[18]

A legal services organization, for example, may designate a special office to serve handicapped clients, if the office is physically accessible and has lawyers trained in handicap law. But it would be unfair to require all handicapped clients, regardless of their legal problems or handicaps, to use only that special office.

Communication barriers. The general nondiscrimination provisions in the HEW regulation apply to the communication barriers faced by deaf people as well as to physical barriers to people in wheelchairs. A deaf woman may be able to walk up a flight of stairs to a job counseling center without difficulty. But if she cannot understand the intake worker's explanations about filling out the forms, she will not be able to do it correctly. She will not know what services are available or how to get them. A deaf man may be able to walk into a hospital or mental health center; but if he cannot communicate with the doctor or counselor, he does not have meaningful, equivalent access to the program and facilities.

The analysis of the HEW regulation gives an example of a welfare office that has a telephone.[19] Clients can call the office for information or to reach caseworkers. Staff can call clients to schedule appointments. But this office must also provide an alternative means to communicate with its deaf clients. The best example of such an alternative would be a TDD-equipped telephone.

Communication problems are specifically addressed in an HEW guideline which requires recipients to take appropriate steps to ensure that communications with applicants, employees, and beneficiaries are available to people with impaired vision and hearing.[20] The "appropriate steps" and "availability" depend on the particular communication situation, but the most common accommodations for hearing-impaired people are qualified sign language interpreters, TDD-equipped telephones, and telephone amplifiers.

Program accessibility. The regulation requires that programs be operated so that handicapped people can use them easily and have equal opportunity to benefit from them.[21] This is called "program accessibility." For people in wheelchairs, this means removing architectural and physical barriers. For deaf people, it means removing communication barriers. Deaf people do not have equal access to—they cannot fully utilize—programs and facilities in which they cannot communicate effectively with the people operating them. Programs and facilities must be "usable" by handicapped people. This requirement of the Rehabilitation Act suggests much more than physical accessibility to a site or building. In effect, the act requires that handicapped people have functionally equivalent services and programs. As a policy concept, "program accessibility" should be invoked aggressively to help deaf people overcome their isolation and exclusion from many programs and services.

The government regulation lists methods to make programs accessible.[22] While the list does not provide much guidance for making specific programs accessible to deaf people, the phrase "re-design of equipment" encompasses modifications to telephones and auditory alarm systems; captions for films and videotapes; and stage, podium, and audiovisual system designs that include facilities and lighting for interpreters. The phrase "assignment of aides" can be interpreted to mean the provision of appropriate interpreters, notetakers, or other aides needed by deaf people. Because the list of methods in the

regulation is not inclusive, deaf and handicapped people should feel free to request any other method that makes programs and activities accessible.

Accessible Meetings

An example of program accessibility is a new HHS regulation for accessible meetings.[23] This regulation establishes not only physical accessibility standards for meetings, seminars, conferences, and other events sponsored by HHS but also necessary service requirements to ensure that sensory-impaired people can participate fully. The regulation specifically lists notetakers, trained interpreters (with adequate lighting to enable them to be seen), and volume-controlled and TDD-equipped telephones.

Interpreters should be available for any meeting, class, or other group activity held by an agency that receives federal financial assistance. Section 504 requires interpreters for cultural events, city government meetings, adult education classes, park programs, or any other event that deaf people may wish to attend. Publicity for meetings should announce the availability of special services and interpreters and should describe the procedures for requesting them.

The needs of deaf people are specifically addressed by one HHS regulation which requires funding recipients to ensure that people with impaired vision or hearing can obtain information about the various services that are accessible to them.[24] For example, incoming telephone lines for inquiries must be TDD-equipped and be identified as such in the recipient's directory listing, letterhead, and anywhere else that the recipient's telephone number is given. Televised public service announcements should be signed or captioned. If programs or services are announced by radio, a recipient might ensure that hearing-impaired people receive the same information by direct mail or by announcements inserted in local newsletters or newspapers distributed by clubs or associations of hearing-impaired people.

Enforcement of Section 504

A handicapped person who believes that a recipient of federal financial assistance has discriminated against him or her on the basis of the handicap has several alternative procedures for seeking redress.

Administrative enforcement. There is no central enforcement mechanism for Section 504. Although the Department of Justice has overall supervision, every agency that provides federal financial assistance is required to adopt its own enforcement procedures as well as its own substantive regulation. Each agency must make its recipients sign assurances of compliance with Section 504 and use the same enforcement procedures as those established to enforce Title VI of the Civil Rights Act of 1964.[25] Within this framework, the procedures used by the various agencies can differ substantially. However, most of the agencies have adopted procedures that are modeled on those developed by HEW and now used by the Departments of Education and of Health and Human Services.

Self-evaluation. All recipients must conduct a self-evaluation of their Section 504 compliance, assisted by interested people including handicapped people or organizations representing them.[26] Recipients of HEW funding were given until June 3, 1978, to complete their self-evaluations, modify any policies or practices that were not in compliance with Section 504, and take appropriate remedial steps to eliminate the effects of any discrimination that resulted from past policies and practices.[27] If a recipient has not yet conducted a self-evaluation or made appropriate modifications, a person bringing a complaint against it can use this mechanism to focus attention on discriminatory practices. If a recipient refuses to conduct a self-evaluation, any interested person can file a complaint asking the appropriate federal agency to compel compliance.

Internal grievance procedure. The Departments of Education and of Health and Human Services require recipients with fifteen or more employees to adopt grievance procedures for complaints alleging discrimination under Section 504. Such recipients must also designate at least one person to coordinate Section 504 compliance. The grievance procedure must incorporate appropriate due process standards and provide for "prompt and equitable" resolution of complaints.[28] Complaint procedures need not be established for applicants seeking employment or admission to postsecondary institutions.

A grievance procedure can be a useful, inexpensive mechanism to resolve simple complaints, especially those stemming from ignorance or misunderstandings about handicaps and Section 504 obligations. Correspondence, memoranda, and other documents generated in grievance proceedings can be used later as evidence of the recipient's discriminatory attitudes or policies. Because the grievance procedure is set up and operated by the recipient itself, though, it will usually be ineffective to resolve major or contested complaints.

Complaint to the federal agency. A handicapped person, or other interested person who believes that a recipient of federal financial assistance has violated

Section 504, can file a complaint with the federal agency that provided the financial assistance. Complaints against recipients of funding from agencies of the Departments of Education or of Health and Human Services should be filed with that agency's regional Office for Civil Rights. The appropriate regional office is that region in which the recipient is located.

Filing Complaints

Complaints must be filed within 180 days of the alleged discriminatory act. For example, if a deaf person went to a hospital on February 1, 1982, and did not get an interpreter, the person must send a complaint to HHS by August 1, 1982. If he or she waits longer than that, the department will not be required to do anything about the complaint. However, the time for filing can be extended at the discretion of the department. Many discriminatory acts are continuous; they represent a general policy or course of conduct. When this is the case, the 180-day limit is not a problem. If there is any doubt whether the time period has elapsed, the complainant should try to use the program or service again—re-apply for benefits or employment, or renew the request for auxiliary aids—so there will be no question that the discriminatory act took place within the time limits.

The complaint can be a simple letter which merely notifies the federal agency of an alleged discriminatory act. However, it will have more impact if it sets out all of the important facts of the discrimination and fully identifies the parts of the Section 504 regulation that have been violated.

The complaint should include the following information:

1. The name, address, and telephone number of the person lodging the complaint ("complainant"), and any special instructions for telephoning a deaf complainant;

2. The name, address, and telephone number of complainant's attorney or other representative, if any;

3. A statement that the complainant is a "qualified handicapped person" under Section 504;

4. The name, address, and telephone number of the program or facility that discriminated and a statement that this program receives financial assistance from the federal agency;

5. A complete description of the discriminatory acts, in chronological order; (The complaint should be as specific as possible about the dates, places, names, and titles of the people involved. The complainant should also explain why the conduct was discriminatory and how the complainant was qualified for the job, benefit, service, or program.)

6. A description of any attempts to complain about the discrimination and the organization's response;

7. Any other information or documents that help explain the discrimination and describe what happened;

8. A list of witnesses, including names, addresses, titles, and telephone numbers; and

9. If possible, an analysis of the parts of the Section 504 regulation that have been violated.

Any relevant documents should be photocopied and attached to the complaint. Do not send original documents. Any attached documents should be numbered and clearly identified by number in the text of the complaint.

Agency Investigation

The federal agency will then investigate to determine whether there has been a violation of Section 504. Agency investigators should interview the complainant, representatives of the program, and other relevant witnesses. The complainant is not a formal "party" to the investigation. The complainant should try to be actively involved in the investigation, however, to make sure that the federal investigator has contacted important witnesses and is familiar with the issues raised by the complaint. This is particularly important in Section 504 complaints involving deafness. Because few investigators are knowledgeable about deafness and the types of auxiliary aids or reasonable accommodations that may be necessary to overcome communication barriers, the investigator may need to meet with experts or other people who can provide relevant information.

If the federal agency finds that a recipient has violated Section 504, it will notify the complainant and the recipient in writing. It will then try to negotiate with the recipient to provide the appropriate relief. The agency can require the recipient to take necessary remedial action to overcome effects of the discrimination.[29] Remedial action can include reinstatement of employees. The agency can also require a remedial action plan that shows what steps the recipient will take within a specific time period to come into compliance. The plan requires the recipient to document its efforts. If the recipient fails to take the required corrective steps, or if negotiations do not result in

a satisfactory resolution, the federal agency will then institute enforcement proceedings to terminate federal financial assistance to the recipient.

Judicial Enforcement

A person has the right to bypass Section 504 agency complaint procedures by bringing a lawsuit in federal court. Investigations by federal agencies can take a long time; by the time they are finished, it may be too late to help the handicapped person. A lawsuit in federal court can often provide a quicker and more effective remedy; and, if the person wins, attorney's fees and other court costs can be awarded. A deaf woman who was about to have a baby found out that her hospital would not allow an interpreter in the delivery room. She could not wait for HEW to investigate her complaint, so she filed a lawsuit in federal court and got immediate help. Federal injunctions have also been upheld in cases involving college students needing classroom interpreters on short notice.

Each of these methods to enforce Section 504 should be reviewed carefully to determine which will be most effective in a particular case.

Notes

1. 29 *United States Code* §791

2. 29 U.S.C. §792

3. 29 U.S.C. §793

4. 29 U.S.C. §794

5. Ibid.

6. Executive Order No. 11,914 (1976), printed in 41 *Federal Register* 17,871, April 28, 1976.

7. 45 *Code of Federal Regulations* §84

8. 45 C.F.R. §84.3(h)

9. 5 U.S.C. §552

10. 45 C.F.R. §84.2

11. 31 U.S.C. §1242(a)(2); 31 C.F.R. §51.52(c)

12. 45 C.F.R. §84.3(j)

13. 45 C.F.R. §84.3(k)

14. 45 C.F.R. §84.4(b)(1)(i)

15. 45 C.F.R. §84.4(b)(1)(ii and iii)

16. 45 C.F.R. §84.4(b)(2)

17. 42 Fed. Reg. 22,676 (1977)

18. 45 C.F.R. §84.4(b)(3)

19. 42 Fed. Reg. 22,687 (1977)

20. 28 C.F.R. §41.51(e)

21. 45 C.F.R. §84.22(a)

22. 45 C.F.R. §84.22(b)

23. 45 Fed. Reg. 25,394 (1980)

24. 45 C.F.R. §84.22(f)

25. 28 C.F.R. §41.5

26. 28 C.F.R. §41.5(b)(2)

27. 45 C.F.R. §84.6(c)

28. 45 C.F.R. §84.7

29. 45 C.F.R. §84.6(a)(1)

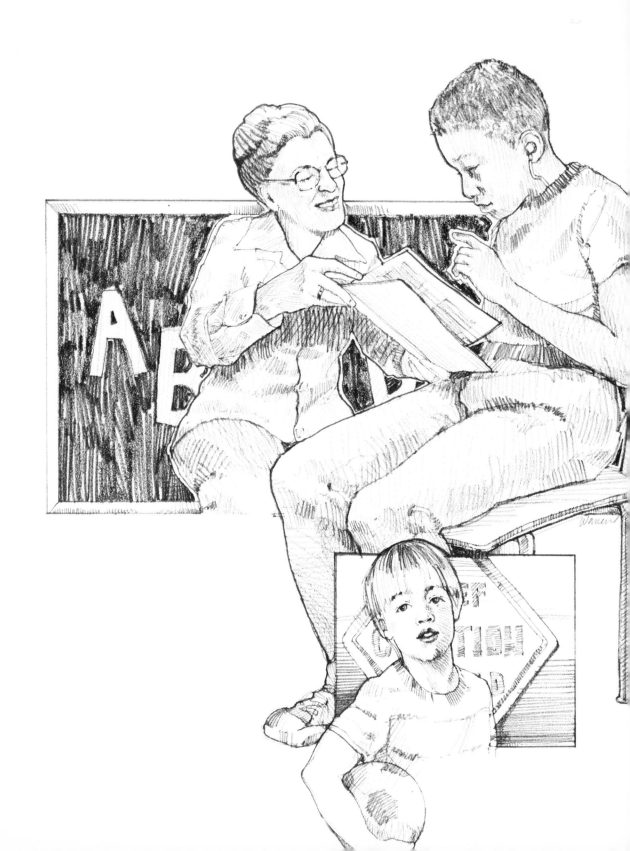

CHAPTER THREE
Public School Education

In these days, it is doubtful that any child may reasonably be expected to succeed in life if he is denied the opportunity of an education. Such an opportunity, where the state has undertaken to provide it, is a right which must be made available to all on equal terms.

Brown v. Board of Education[1]

The *Brown* case was decided in 1954, but many handicapped children are still denied their right to equal educational opportunity. In 1975 Congress found that more than half of this nation's eight million handicapped children were not receiving appropriate educational services, and one million were excluded from the public school system entirely.[2] Congress has enacted several laws, discussed in this chapter, that guarantee handicapped children the right to qualified teachers, accessible classrooms, and appropriate materials and programs.

Section 504 of the Rehabilitation Act of 1973 applies, among other things, to school systems and educational agencies that receive federal financial assistance. Like all other institutions that receive federal money, schools are prohibited from discriminating against handicapped people. Their programs must be accessible to and usable by handicapped people. In the Department of Education's Section 504 regulation, public elementary and secondary schools are required to provide a "free, appropriate public education" to qualified handicapped children, regardless of the nature of their handicap.[3]

This means that, if the local school system does not have appropriate teachers or programs to educate a child, it must send the child to another school that does, paying the child's

Parts of this chapter and Chapters Four, Five, Seven, and Nine are adapted from S. DuBow and S. Geer, "Communications Barriers." In P. Hearne, ed., *Legal Advocacy for the Handicapped: A Legal Services Practical Manual* (Washington, D.C.: Legal Services Corp., 1981), chapter 3. Used by permission of the publisher.

tuition if the school is private. The school system cannot make the child's parents pay for any of the special services the child needs. If the school system refuses to provide an appropriate education to a handicapped child, ED can cut off federal funds.

Public Law 94-142

Congress passed another law in 1975 that is more specific about the education of handicapped children. This law is Public Law 94-142, the Education for All Handicapped Children Act.[4] It is similar to Section 504 in that it requires public school systems to give handicapped children a free, appropriate public education. But this law is more comprehensive than the education provisions of Section 504. It provides the states with money for special education and imposes clear procedural and substantive requirements on how that special education should be provided. Regulations implementing PL 94-142 were adopted in 1977.

The law and its regulations are intended to fulfill four major purposes:

- to ensure that all handicapped children have available to them a free, appropriate public education which emphasizes special education and related services designed to meet their unique needs;
- to ensure that the rights of handicapped children and their parents or guardians are protected;
- to help states and localities pay for

the education of all handicapped children;
- and to ensure and assess the effectiveness of the educational programs.[5]

The rest of this chapter will discuss the specific requirements of PL 94-142 as they relate to the education of deaf children and to some of the parallel requirements of Section 504. In addition to these two federal laws, most states

---

Under PL 94-142

- "Deaf" means a hearing impairment which is so severe that the child is impaired in processing linguistic information through hearing, with or without amplification, which adversely affects educational performance.

- "Deaf-blind" means concomitant hearing and visual impairments, the combination of which causes such severe communication and other developmental and educational problems that they cannot be accommodated in special education programs solely for deaf or blind children.

- "Hard of hearing" means a hearing impairment, permanent or fluctuating, which adversely affects a child's educational performance but which is not included under the definition of "deaf" in this section.[6]

---

have adopted their own laws or regulations to go along with the PL 94-142 requirements. They usually give handicapped children similar educational rights under state law and establish procedures for getting special education services that meet the standards of PL 94-142.

The handicapped children protected by PL 94-142 are defined in very specific terms. The law covers children who need special education and related services because of their handicaps. The list includes children who are mentally retarded, hard-of-hearing, deaf, speech-impaired, visually handicapped, seriously emotionally disturbed, orthopedically impaired, deaf-blind, multihandicapped, or who have other health impairments and specific learning disabilities.

Appropriate Education

The heart of the law is the guaranteed right of every child to a free, appropriate education. Under PL 94-142 and Section 504, every handicapped child has a right to (1) specially designed instruction to meet his or her unique needs and (2) related services that may be necessary to help the child benefit from the special program. Moreover, this education must take place in the least restrictive environment. Public Law 94-142 requires states to ensure that, to the maximum extent possible, handicapped children are educated with children who are not handicapped. Special classes

and separate school placements are appropriate only when the handicap is of such a nature or severity that placement in regular classes with the use of supplementary aids and services will not meet the educational needs of that child satisfactorily. The physical integration of handicapped and nonhandicapped children in school classrooms is called "mainstreaming."*

Mainstreaming can reduce the stigma and isolation for many handicapped children, but it is not always appropriate for deaf children. Without substantial support systems and services, the assignment into a classroom of hearing children constitutes a more socially and educationally restrictive environment than a setting in which the students and teachers have a shared language. The individual child's specific needs must govern any decision about his or her program.

The Individualized Education Program

Under PL 94-142 a school system must devise an appropriate Individualized Education Program (IEP) for each handicapped child. The IEP is a written report that identifies and assesses the

---

*See Appendix A for a reference list of publications on deafness and PL 94-142, including a special section on publications which deal with mainstreaming.

child's disability, establishes long- and short-term learning goals, and states which services the school must provide to help the child achieve them. Special education and related services are then provided in accordance with the terms of the IEP.

A school violates PL 94-142 if it draws up an IEP and merely presents it to parents for their consent. Parents work with school officials to develop it. The meetings where this work is done can also include the child's current teacher, a representative of the school system who is qualified to provide or

supervise the special services, the child (where appropriate), and other people at the discretion of the parents or the school.[7] Parents may ask professional and legal experts to attend the meeting. If the parents are deaf, the law specifically requires that the school system provide an interpreter so they can participate fully in the meeting. Before the IEP meeting, the parents should exercise their right to review, without cost to them, their child's school records to make sure that the information is accurate and complete.

Public Law 94-142 says that parents must be involved in the identification, evaluation, and placement decisions involving handicapped children and that no child can be placed in a special education program without parental consent. The law requires that parents be fully informed about placement and educational decisions affecting a child and consent to the initial programs and later changes in placement.[8]

The IEP must include:

1. A statement of the child's present levels of educational performance.

2. A statement of annual goals, including short-term instructional objectives.

3. A statement of the specific special education and related services to be provided to the child, and the extent to which the child will be able to participate in regular educational programs.

4. The projected dates for initiation of services and anticipated duration of the services.

5. Appropriate objective criteria and evaluation procedures and schedules for determining, on at least an annual basis, whether the short-term instructional objectives are being achieved.[9]

The goals and objectives that are written into the IEP are not limited to academic performance. The goals should relate to social, psychomotor, communication, and emotional needs as well as to conventional academic curriculum goals.

The IEP is the critical mechanism whereby parents may make certain that their child receives an appropriate education. The school is legally required to provide the services that are written into the IEP. Parents should be certain that it includes every special service that the child needs. They should not sign an IEP that does not specify in great detail the services they believe the child needs in order to benefit from a special education. Parents who disagree with the proposed service plan, have any complaints, or are unconvinced that the school has the necessary resources should not sign the IEP. They instead should initiate due process procedures (discussed later).

Parents should ask for and keep a copy of their child's IEP so they can remember what was agreed upon and hold the school to its promises. If they later have to go to court to obtain the services, the IEP will be the primary item of evidence.

The IEP must be worded to ensure the deaf child's access to communication in the classroom. Some hearing-impaired children benefit from having supplementary hearing devices that range from conventional hearing aids to specialized auditory training devices and amplification equipment. Besides these, a child may need special services to increase use of residual hearing. These services should be specified in the IEP and provided as part of the child's program.

For example, control of background noise may be essential if a child is to receive the full benefit of a hearing aid. If so, this need should be identified so the school can take appropriate steps to improve acoustics. Improved lighting may be necessary to ensure that information presented visually is clear and understandable. Speech therapy, auditory training, and media support services (such as captioned TV and films) are other related services that a deaf child might need; if so, these services should be written into the IEP.

Public Law 94-142 specifically mentions these related services: transportation, speech pathology, audiology, psychological services, physical and occupational therapy, recreation, counseling services, and medical services for diagnostic or evaluation purposes.

Supreme Court Decision

In June 1982 the U.S. Supreme Court decided its first case involving PL 94-142. The case was *Hendrick Hudson School District v. Rowley*.[10] Lower courts had ruled that Amy Rowley, a mainstreamed elementary school student, required a sign language interpreter to make classroom instruction fully accessible. The Supreme Court affirmed the right of all handicapped children to receive personalized instruction and the support services they need to benefit from their educational program. In Rowley's particular case, however, the Court found that she

did not need an interpreter because she was doing well in school without one. She was receiving sufficient other support services, said the Court, to enable her to benefit from her education (e.g., a phonic ear listening device and a personal tutor).

This does not mean that other deaf children will be unable to get interpreter services or total communication programs. It merely means they must show that they cannot benefit from their education without such a service. Amy's lipreading skills, residual hearing, and high intelligence made her a special case.

A majority of the Court found that Congress did not intend to give handicapped children a right to "strict equality of opportunity or services" because that would require impossible measurements and comparisons. But PL 94-142 does require access to a free, appropriate public education for handicapped children that is "meaningful." The Court held that a state " . . . satisfies this requirement by providing personalized instruction with sufficient supportive services to permit the child to benefit educationally from that instruction."

The Court upheld the major purposes of PL 94-142 as outlined on page 28. The IEP and the due process hearing for parents were not changed. They remain at the heart of the law and continue to give parents the opportunity to prove that their child needs a particular service or program.

Writing the IEP

In the case of deaf children, the statutory mandate of a free and appropriate public education poses unusual and controversial problems that affect the writing of the IEP. An emotional and sometimes bitter historical debate exists concerning the best methods for teaching deaf children. Many professionals are firm proponents of one method or another, which complicates the task of a parent or attorney seeking expert guidance in formulating a child's IEP.

In addition to the four primary methods of instruction (see box), "total communication" has received wide attention in recent years. Perhaps the best definition of the term comes from

---

Four primary methods of instruction currently used in the United States are described by D. F. Moores:

1. Oral method. In this system, also called the oral-aural method, children receive input through speechreading (lipreading) and amplification of sound, and they express themselves through speech. Gestures and signs are prohibited.

2. Auditory method. This approach, as opposed to the oral, is basically unsensory. It concentrates on developing listening skills in children, who are expected to rely primarily on hearing. Early reading and writing are discouraged, as is a dependence on speechreading or signs. Although this method was developed for children with moderate hearing losses, some attempts have been made to use it with profoundly impaired children.

3. Rochester method. This is a combination of the oral method plus fingerspelling. Children receive information through speechreading, amplification, and fingerspelling, and they express themselves through speech and fingerspelling. Reading and writing usually receive great emphasis. The proficient teacher spells every letter of every word in coordination with speech and can present at the rate of approximately one hundred words per minute. The system of neo-oralism developed in the Soviet Union also utilizes speech and fingerspelling.

4. Simultaneous method. This is a combination of the oral method plus signs and fingerspelling. The children receive input through speechreading, amplification, signs, and fingerspelling. They express themselves in speech, signs, and fingerspelling. Signs are differentiated from fingerspelling in that they may represent complete ideas or words rather than standing for individual letters of the English alphabet.[11]

---

the Conference of Executives of American Schools for the Deaf: "Total communication is a philosophy incorporating appropriate aural, manual, and oral modes of communication in order to ensure effective communication with and among hearing-impaired persons."[12]

Appropriate Language Medium

Any consideration of educational methods using manual components is complicated by the existence of sign language dialects and by the number of different possible systems for using manual language with children in a learning setting. "Sign language" is a continuum of language systems that can be differentiated by the types of visual components (signs, fingerspelling, body movement, and facial expression) used and by the degree to which a particular system parallels formal English syntax and vocabulary.

American Sign Language (ASL) is linguistically independent of English. However, a number of other systems used in schools are closely related to English. They have been devised to "make English visible" by providing word-by-word translation of English through use of signs and fingerspelling, with additional signs to represent word endings and other grammatical forms. Cued speech is another method that has been introduced in some school systems in recent years. The method is not a language but a system of handshapes made near the mouth which represent phonemes of English. The child lipreads while simultaneously reading the manual cues.

In determining the proper educational program for a hearing-impaired child and in writing the IEP, the critical first step is to identify the language medium that is appropriate for that child. What is best varies from child to child, depending on his or her native language, the amount and type of residual hearing (if any), the level of the child's communication skills, his or her exposure to manual communication methods, age of onset of deafness, and other conditions. What is found to be appropriate should be spelled out in the IEP.

Selecting the proper communication medium is important because it makes instruction possible and meaningful. All educators of deaf children are concerned with maximizing the child's speaking and understanding of the English language. A related but more immediate goal is to make what happens in the classroom accessible to that child. With some children, this might mean providing only a hearing aid; other children will require both an aid and a sign language interpreter; and still others will need a special teacher and a range of support services. The IEP should spell out the individual's requirements.

Experienced Professionals

Childhood deafness is a low-incidence disability. Most school

systems have relatively few deaf
children in each age group, a factor that
increases the difficulty of providing
properly trained teachers and highly
specialized, related services to ensure
an appropriate education in mainstream classes.

A 1976 position paper of the International Association of Parents of the
Deaf noted:

> Currently, many local and public
> schools lack qualified diagnostic staff
> for making the placement, lack sup-
> portive services, lack trained person-
> nel, lack necessary amplification
> equipment and a desirable visual envi-
> ronment, lack an understanding of
> total communication which may be
> essential for communication with
> students, and in many cases, lack

financial resources required for the
education of deaf children and lack
commitment.[13]

School systems are required by law
to evaluate children for hearing loss, to
create special programs to prevent hearing loss, and to provide counseling
and guidance to students, parents, and
teachers. They are responsible for
determining a child's need for amplification, for selecting and fitting an appropriate aid, and for evaluating the effectiveness of the amplification.[14] These
responsiblities can overwhelm teachers
and administrators who lack special
training. Opportunities for such training must be made available to school
staff so they may become more knowl-

edgeable about deafness and other disabilities, the range of possible solutions and accommodations, and how they may best meet their responsibilities under the law. Inservice training, special certification, and sign language training may be appropriate.

Procedural Safeguards

Both Section 504 and PL 94-142 provide procedural safeguards by which parents can be assured of both their own participation in the decision-making process and an appropriate education for their child.

A school system must give written notice to parents when it wishes to initiate or change the identification, evaluation, or placement of a handicapped child.[15] The notice must describe procedural protections, the action that the school system proposes or refuses to take, and its reasons. The notice must also describe any options the school system considered and explain why those options were rejected. Each evaluation procedure, test, record, report, or other relevant factor the school system used as a basis for the proposal or refusal must be described in the notice.

The notice must be written in language understandable to the general public and provided in the native language of the parent or any other possible form of communication used by the parent. If the native language or form of communication is not a written language, the school system has to translate the notice and ensure that the parent understands it.[16] The notice must be translated and explained to deaf parents by a qualified sign language interpreter.

If the parents do not accept the school system's evaluation and proposed placement or program, or if they are not confident that the school system has the resources to provide an appropriate education, they can request a due process hearing.* They simply notify the school officials that they are dissatisfied, state their reasons, and ask for a hearing. The notification should but does not have to be in writing. The hearing and a final decision must be completed within forty-five days of the request.

The due process hearing is intended to be an informal dispute-resolution process during which both the parents and the school can present their grievances to a neutral hearing officer. Either the parents or the school can request a hearing. A neutral hearing officer is appointed according to procedures established by the state. The hearing officer may not be an employee of the agency or unit involved in the education or care of the child and cannot have any personal or professional interest that would impair his or her objectivity in

---

*See Appendix B for sample letters requesting any of the following: an evaluation of a child's education program, a child's school records, a due process hearing, or a state review.

the hearing. Public agencies must keep a list of hearing officers which states their qualifications.

Preparation for the Hearing

There are several steps to be taken in preparation for the hearing. One essential step is to find experts in education who can testify in support of the parents' position that the placement is inappropriate. The expert should visit the proposed and current placements before the hearing in order to testify whether the proposed placement can meet the specific needs of that individual child. The parents themselves should visit the proposed placement and see how the IEP could be implemented with the school's resources.

The parents also should examine all school records relevant to their child's placement. Under PL 94-142, the school system must comply with any reasonable request by the parents to inspect and receive an explanation of their child's records before any hearing. If the parents believe that information in the file is incorrect, they can request amendment of the record. If the parents disagree with the educational evaluation of their child, they have the right to an independent evaluation; the school system is required to take this evaluation into account in deciding the child's placement. Well before the hearing date, the parents should request a list of witnesses who will be testifying for the school.

Parents have the right to request attendance of their child's proposed classroom teacher, and they should exercise that right. It is essential that the hearing officer be made aware of the teacher's qualifications and that the parents have an opportunity to question how the teacher hopes to implement the individual educational plan for their child. The parents should also request the attendance of teachers from any alternative placement the parents may wish to propose; these teachers can testify as to how they would meet the individual needs of the child.

The key issue at the hearing is whether the proposed placement is appropriate to meet the individual needs of that disabled child. At the hearing, the parents can have a lawyer and can call witnesses who are experts in educating disabled children. They also have the right to present evidence and to confront and cross-examine any of the witnesses.

Parents can obtain a written or electronic verbatim record of the hearing, which is important in an appeal. The hearing officer must provide written findings of fact for his/her decision. Until a decision is rendered, the child must remain in the present educational placement unless the school and the parents agree otherwise. If, however, the complaint involves application for initial admission to public school, the child must be placed in the public school program until completion of all proceedings.

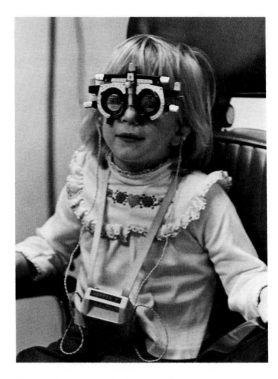

Decisions and Appeals

The hearing officer has the authority to determine the most appropriate placement for the child and is not restricted to merely accepting or rejecting the school's program. The hearing officer can order services that are necessary to provide a free, appropriate education for the child. The decision of the hearing officer is final and must be obeyed by the school system, unless it is appealed to the state department of education or the courts.

If an appeal is made to the state education agency, the agency must conduct an impartial review of the decision. The official who conducts the review must examine the entire hearing record, ensure that the procedures at the hearing were consistent with the due process requirements of the law, seek additional evidence if necessary, afford the parties an opportunity for oral or written argument or both, make an independent decision on completion of the review, and give a copy of written findings and the decision to the parties.

The parents may file a civil lawsuit in state or federal court to challenge the decision of the state agency. Complaints to the federal Department of Education's Office for Civil Rights or the Bureau for Education of the Handicapped may be appropriate if there are systematic violations of Section 504 or PL 94-142 by a school system. If the school system fails to comply with the laws, the federal agency can order the termination of federal funds for the entire system.

School Activities

Public Law 94-142 applies only to deaf and handicapped school children, but some school activities are open to adults as well as to children. Because most school systems receive federal financial assistance, they must obey Section 504 in all their programs. Deaf people must be able to use the programs of the school, even if the deaf person is not a student at that school. For example, many school systems offer continuing education classes for adults or hobby classes that take place in the schools during evenings and

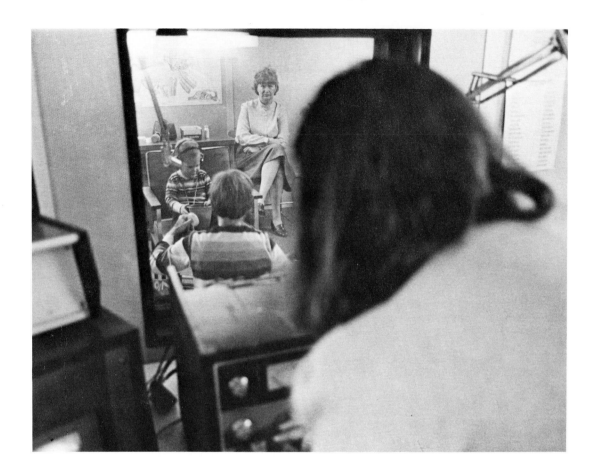

weekends. These programs must be open and accessible to deaf people, and the school should provide interpreters for the deaf students to enable them to participate in the classes.

Schools also should provide interpreters for deaf parents who need them in order to participate in parent-teacher conferences and other school activities involving parents. The provision should be made regardless of whether the child of the deaf parents is also deaf.

Notes

1. 375 U.S. 438 at 493 (1954)

2. 20 *United States Code* §1401

3. 45 *Code of Federal Regulations* §84.33(a)

4. 20 U.S.C. §1401 *et seq.*

5. 34 C.F.R. §300.1

6. 34 C.F.R. §300.5(b)

7. 34 C.F.R. §300.343, 300.344(a)

8. 34 C.F.R. §300.345

9. 34 C.F.R. §300.346

10. 102 S. Ct. 3034 (1982)

11. D. F. Moores, *Educating the Deaf: Psychology, Principles, and Practices,* 2d ed. (Boston: Houghton Mifflin, 1982), p. 9. Used by permission of the publisher.

12. Quoted in Mervin D. Garretson, "Total Communication," in Robert D. Frisina, ed., *A Bicentennial Monograph on Hearing-Impairment: Trends in the U.S.A.* (Washington, D.C.: Alexander Graham Bell Association for the Deaf, 1976), p. 91.

13. International Association of Parents of the Deaf, October 1976 position statement.

14. 34 C.F.R. §300.303

15. 45 C.F.R. §84.36

16. 34 C.F.R. §300.505(b)(1)

CHAPTER FOUR
Postsecondary Education

The Department of Education's regulations for Section 504 help make postsecondary education accessible to disabled people. Basically, the regulation prohibits those institutions which receive federal money, including vocational and commercial schools, from discriminating against disabled people in recruitment, admissions, and programs. To accommodate a disabled person, the institution is not obligated to change substantially the requirements of its academic program; it must, however, afford equal opportunity for the person to benefit from the program, without segregation from the other students or limits on participation. Auxiliary aids are mandated by the regulations, and methods of evaluation are required to measure the student's actual achievement and not his or her ability to take tests.

Recruitment and Admissions

Educational institutions may neither refuse to admit disabled applicants because of their handicap nor subject them to any form of discrimination in admission or recruitment procedures.[1] If the college requires pre-admission interviews of its applicants, deaf applicants must be interviewed too, with interpreters provided. If the college has tours or orientation meetings, the deaf applicant must be able to participate with an interpreter present. If a college sends promotional information or makes recruitment visits to area high schools, then it must do the same for area deaf schools. The institution cannot place a limit or quota on the number or proportion of disabled students who may be admitted.

In addition, the ED regulation prohibits colleges and universities from making pre-admission inquiries about handicaps, except in two situations: (a) when the school is taking remedial action to overcome the effects of past discrimination, or (b) when it is taking voluntary action to overcome the effects of conditions that limited the participation of disabled persons in the school's programs in the past. In either of these circumstances, the school must clearly state that the information sought is intended for use only in connection with remedial or voluntary action. After the student is admitted, the school can make confidential inquiries about handicaps that may require some accommodation.

The Supreme Court has decided a case concerning pre-admission inquiries about a person's handicap. In *Southeastern Community College v. Davis* (discussed later in more detail), the Court held that a nursing school could require "reasonable physical qualifications for admission to a clinical training program" and reject a student whose handicap would require substantial modifications of a program.[2] For other kinds of academic programs, however, the section of the Department of Education regulation concerning pre-admission inquiries was left intact. Except for professional clinical programs, such as the nursing program in the *Davis* case, educational institutions are still prohibited from asking about or considering physical handicap in the admission process.

Educational institutions must ensure that admissions tests are selected and administered so that the test results accurately reflect the applicant's actual aptitude or achievement level and not the effects of his or her hearing impairment.[3] For example, oral instructions should be translated into sign language or put into writing. Oral examinations should be conducted with a qualified sign language interpreter or other appropriate aid. If a test is designed to measure aptitude for or achievement in some area other than English language skills, then the test should be modified for the deaf applicant who does not have standard English skills. More time might be provided or another test, less reliant on English competence, might be used.

Treatment of Students

Disabled students at federally funded colleges must be treated equally with nondisabled students. Programs must be conducted in an integrated setting. Separate facilities for disabled students are not permitted.[4] Recipient institutions must also ensure that other programs in which its disabled students participate do not discriminate. Examples of other programs are internships, clinical placement programs, student teaching assignments, or coursework at other schools in a consortium. The recipient institution may not continue its relationships with any program that in any way discriminates against its disabled students.[5]

Colleges and universities must make adjustments to those requirements that discriminate against a disabled student.[6] For example, a deaf student should be allowed to substitute a music history or art appreciation course for a required course in music appreciation. A college might permit a qualified deaf

student seeking teacher certification to do an internship teaching a class of deaf students in order to meet degree requirements. The individual capabilities and needs of each student must be considered and academic adjustments made as appropriate. Since the *Davis* decision, however, a college is not required to make substantial modifications in its program in order to accommodate handicapped students. Nor is a college required to change those academic requirements that the college can prove are essential either to the program of instruction or for a particular degree.[7]

Auxiliary Aids

Postsecondary institutions must ensure that a handicapped student has any auxiliary aids that are necessary for him or her to fully participate in the educational program.[8] Examples of auxiliary aids in the ED regulation are taped texts, interpreters, readers in libraries, and classroom equipment adapted for use by students with manual impairments. For hearing-impaired students, auxiliary aids include any effective means of making orally-delivered material available to them. In addition to qualified interpreters, these aids might include notetakers or funds for copying the notes of a classmate, since the deaf student must constantly watch the interpreter and instructor and cannot write at the same time. Auxiliary aids might also include transcripts or interpretations of tape-recorded or filmed information and interpretation or captioning of films and videotapes.

A postsecondary educational institution can refer a student to another source for provision of auxiliary aids or try to obtain the necessary auxiliary aids from such outside sources as the local vocational rehabilitation office or charitable groups. However, the school remains responsible for seeing that the aids are received and that they in fact enable the deaf student to participate in the education program. The school has ultimate responsibility to find and pay for interpreters and other auxiliary aids.

Two federal district courts have decided since *Davis* that, for deaf college students who are vocational rehabilitation (VR) clients, the VR agency must

pay for their interpreters. A New Jersey district judge found that it is a VR agency's legal duty to pay for interpreters based on Title I of the Rehabilitation Act. An Illinois district court judge held that when a student is a VR client, the state VR agency has primary responsibility under Section 504 to pay for interpreter services for the student's classes.

The Two Cases

Ruth Ann Schornstein is a deaf VR client who attends Kean College in New Jersey. Her plan is to earn a college degree in social work/psychology. The New Jersey Division of Vocational Rehabilitation Services accepted Ms. Schornstein as an eligible VR client and developed an individual rehabilitation plan to meet her vocational goal. Although the state agency provided tuition and books, they refused to provide interpreter services. All groups involved agreed she needs an interpreter to participate effectively in her classes. The court later found that without the interpreter these other benefits will be useless.

The National Association of the Deaf Legal Defense Fund (NADLDF) filed a lawsuit against both the state agency and Kean College. The federal court held that the state agency's policy denying interpreter services to every deaf college student violates Title I of the Rehabilitation Act. Title I requires state VR agencies to provide certain rehabilitation services, including interpreters, to accepted VR clients. The federal court ruled that the state agency policy "completely contradicts the Acts's requirements which ensure individualization of programs for handicapped individuals."

The state agency argued that it could decide what services to provide. The court was not persuaded. It found that the Rehabilitation Act specifically requires VR agencies to (1) serve severely handicapped individuals, including deaf people, first; and (2) provide those services listed in the Rehabilitation Act which are necessary to assist the handicapped person to achieve his or her vocational goal.

Because the state agency accepted Schornstein as a client and also agreed that she requires interpreter services to meet her vocational goals, the court concluded that the agency is legally obligated to provide those services. Since the court decided the case solely on the basis of Title I, it did not find it necessary to rule on the obligation to provide interpreters under either Section 504 or the U.S. Constitution.

The case helps clarify the responsibility of VR agencies to provide interpreters to deaf VR clients attending college.[9]

In the Illinois case, a deaf student majoring in mechanical engineering at the Illinois Institute of Technology (IIT) in Chicago, Illinois, needed an interpreter in order to understand and participate in his classes, which began in August 1979. Although he was an eligible VR client—receiving tuition, room and board, and books from the

Illinois Department of Rehabilitation Services—the VR agency refused to provide him with interpreters. He was also refused these interpreter services by the college.

The court stated that when a student is a VR client, the state VR agency has primary responsibility under Section 504 to pay for interpreter services for the student's classes. The court went on to say that if the student is not a VR client, and no other sources are available, then the college has the ultimate responsibility to pay for interpreter services.

The Illinois VR agency tried unsuccessfully to persuade the court that it

was prohibited from providing interpreters to the student under Title I, if other "similar benefit" programs or community resources were available to pay for these services. The VR agency claimed that the college had a legal obligation under Section 504 to provide interpreters to deaf students. As a "similar benefit" program or community resource, the college, said the VR agency, should have to pay for interpreters. The court found that only other rehabilitation services were intended by Congress to be "similar benefit" programs.[10] The Illinois rehabilitation agency has appealed this decision.

Other Legal Precedents

The Department of Education and, before it, the Department of Health, Education, and Welfare have issued findings of violation against several colleges and universities for not providing interpreter services for deaf students.[11]

Courts have also found illegal the refusal of colleges and universities to provide interpreters.[12] In *Camenisch v. University of Texas*, the Fifth Circuit Court of Appeals upheld a district court's preliminary injunction requiring the University of Texas to provide an interpreter to a deaf graduate student.[13] The court also ruled that disabled people have a right to sue in federal court to enforce their Section 504 rights. Furthermore, said the court, a disabled person did not first have to exhaust administrative remedies before bringing a lawsuit.

The university appealed to the Supreme Court. After accepting the case, the Court refused to decide the Section 504 issues raised by the university.[14] Instead, it sent the case back to the district court to decide whether the university or Camenisch had to pay for the interpreter. The Court held that the university had only appealed a preliminary injunction order and had not waited for a trial on the merits. The Court found the case moot, because the terms of the preliminary injunction had been fulfilled with Camenisch being provided an interpreter and having already graduated.

The Supreme Court's first ruling on the merits of a case brought under Section 504 was the *Davis* case. The issue was whether Section 504 "forbids professional schools from imposing physical qualifications for admission to their clinical training programs."[15] In its decision, the court also sought to clarify the meaning of "qualified handicapped individual" in postsecondary education and the extent of affirmative relief required by Section 504.

Frances Davis, a licensed practical nurse with a hearing impairment, sought to enroll in a nursing school program to become a registered nurse. Despite evidence that she could perform well in this program, Southeastern Community College rejected Davis's application because of her hearing loss.

The district court upheld the college's decision, noting that in settings such as an operating room, intensive care unit, or postnatal care unit, the wearing of surgical masks would prevent Davis from reading lips to understand what was happening. The district court concluded that Davis's "handicap actually prevents her from safely performing in both her training program and her proposed profession."[16]

The Court of Appeals for the Fourth Circuit reversed the decision. In light of the HEW Section 504 regulation (issued after the district court's decision), the appeals court ruled that the college had to reconsider Davis's application without regard to her hearing disability.[17] The appeals court concluded that the district court erred in considering the nature of Davis's disability to determine whether she was "otherwise qualified" for the program rather than limiting its inquiry to her "academic and technical qualifications," which is the requirement of the regulation. Because the college said that it was not prepared to modify its nursing program to accommodate Davis's hearing disability, the appeals court sent the case back to the district court for it to consider what modifications required by the HEW regulation might accommodate Davis.

Supreme Court Decision

The Supreme Court agreed to review the case and found unanimously that the college had not violated Section 504. The Court held that:

> Nothing in the language or history of §504 reflects the intention to limit the freedom of an educational institution to require reasonable physical qualifi-

cations for admission to a clinical training program. Nor has there been any showing in this case that any action short of a substantial change in Southeastern's program would render unreasonable the qualifications it imposed.[18]

Writing for the Court, Justice Lewis Powell found that Section 504 does not compel schools to disregard an applicant's disabilities "or to make *substantial* modifications in their programs to allow disabled persons to participate" (our emphasis).[19] Instead, the Court interpreted Section 504 to mean that mere possession of a handicap is not a permissible ground for assuming an inability to function in a particular context.[20]

The Court also found that, under Section 504, an "otherwise handicapped person" is "one who is able to meet all of a program's requirements in spite of his handicap."[21] Davis was considered unable to meet those requirements since "the ability to understand speech without reliance on lipreading is necessary for patient safety during the clinical phase of the program."[22] The Court stated that, on the basis of meager evidence contained in the trial record, it was unlikely that Davis could successfully participate in the clinical program with any of the accommodations the regulation requires. The Court concluded that either close individual supervision or changing the curriculum to limit her participation to academic classes exceeded the "modification" required by the regulation.

The Court noted, however, that continuing some requirements may wrongly exclude qualified disabled people from participating in programs:

> Thus situations may arise where a refusal to modify an existing program might become unreasonable and discriminatory. Identification of these instances where a refusal to accommodate the needs of a disabled person amounts to discrimination against the handicapped continues to be an important responsibility of HEW.[23]

The Court's ruling that Section 504 does not require substantial program modification has led some states and schools to oppose any modifications on grounds of undue costs. The Court's decision was limited to professional clinical programs, but some recipient institutions are using it as an excuse not to provide interpreters in purely academic programs.

The ruling also poses a danger that schools will set physical qualifications

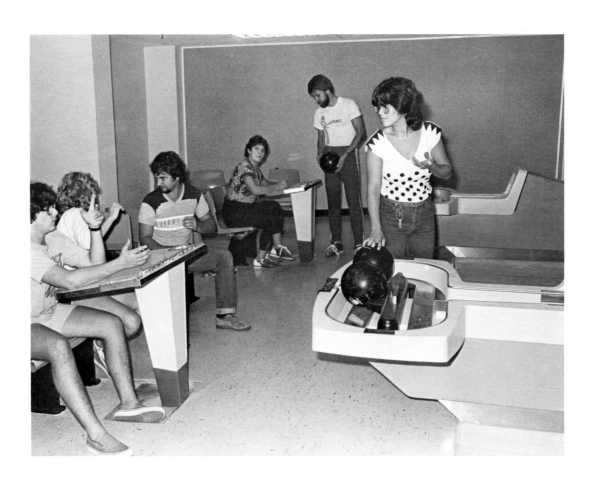

allowing only able-bodied students, or disabled students not in need of any accommodation, to be admitted; schools might argue that these are legitimate "technical" requirements for admission. Future Department of Education and court decisions will address issues of whether proposed modifications are "substantial" and whether physical qualifications are "reasonable" and "necessary."

Complete Trial Records

The Supreme Court showed a lack of sensitivity to the capabilities and contributions of disabled people, as evidenced by Justice Powell's remark that "technological advances may qualify handicapped people for *some useful*

employment" (our emphasis).[24] In order to better sensitize the Court in this new area of disability law, and to persuade it in future cases to take a more inclusive view of the rights of disabled people, a full trial record is necessary. As mentioned, the trial record in the *Davis* case was incomplete and contained no information on either Davis's capabilities or what accommodations might be made. The case was sent back to the lower court for a determination of her qualifications.

In future cases, an adequate trial record should be developed by having the disabled person testify about his or her qualifications and capabilities and the accommodations that are required. Other disabled people who have successfully participated in similar programs or who are practicing in related careers should testify in order to remove any presumption that disabled people cannot perform particular functions effectively. They can also suggest possible accommodations. Finally, experts in the applicant's particular field should testify as to what aspects of a program are essential to that field and how program modifications can be made without lowering any of the school's standards.

In the future, a case should not be appealed without a strong trial record. Also, it is important at the lower court stage to obtain legal assistance from attorneys who specialize in disability law and/or from the Justice Department's impact litigation unit.

Notes

1. 45 *Code of Federal Regulations* §84.42

2. Southeastern Community College v. Davis, 442 U.S. 397 at 414 (1979)

3. 45 C.F.R. §84.42(b)(3)

4. 45 C.F.R. §84.43(d)

5. 45 C.F.R. §84.43(b)

6. 45 C.F.R. §84.44(a)

7. 42 *Federal Register* 22,692 (1977)

8. 45 C.F.R. §84.44(d)

9. Schornstein v. The New Jersey Division of Vocational Rehabilitation Services, 519 *Federal Supplement* 773 (D.N.J. 1981), affirmed 688 F.2d 824 (3d Cir. 1982) (mem.)

10. Jones v. Illinois Department of Rehabilitation Services, 504 F. Supp. 1244 (N.D. Ill. 1981), affirmed 689 F.2d 724 (7th Cir. 1982)

11. Manley v. Patterson College, Docket No. 79-0001 NE (Region II); Warso v. Southern Florida University, Docket No. 0419780109 (Region IV); and Arnold v. University of Alabama at Birmingham, Docket No. 04107902090 (Region IV).

12. Crawford v. University of North Carolina, 440 F. Supp. 1047 (M.D.N.C. 1977); Herbold v. Trustees of the California State Universities and Colleges, C-78-1358-RHS (N.D. Cal. 1978); and Barnes v. Converse College, 436 F. Supp. 635 (D.S.C. 1977).

13. 616 F.2d 127 (5th Cir. 1980)

14. Camenisch v. University of Texas, 451 U.S. 390 (1981)

15. Southeastern Community College v. Davis, 442 U.S. 397 at 400 (1979)

16. 424 F. Supp. 1341 at 1345

17. 574 F.2d 1158 (4th Cir., 1978)

18. 442 U.S. 397 at 414

19. 442 U.S. 397 at 405

20. Ibid.

21. 442 U.S. 397 at 406

22. 442 U.S. 397 at 407

23. 442 U.S. 397 at 412–413

24. 442 U.S. 397 at 412

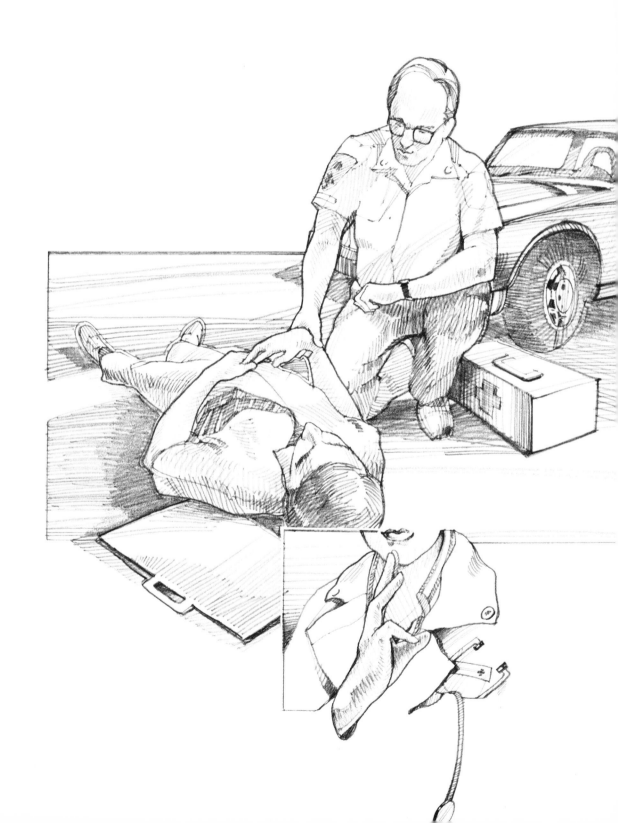

CHAPTER FIVE
Health Care and Social Services

Most communities have a complicated network of public and private agencies that provide important social and health services. Many of these agencies receive significant federal assistance and must therefore comply with Section 504 of the 1973 Rehabilitation Act. They are not allowed to discriminate against disabled people.

This does not mean that deaf people find it easy to get the services to which they are entitled. They are sometimes turned away from a program simply because no one on the staff can communicate with them or understand what they need. Deaf people often get little or no service in situations where hearing people receive good service. A hearing person may get answers to questions about food stamp eligibility, for example, or advice on how to complete an application or information on the details of a program. But the deaf person may be handed a standard written form with cursory explanations of

office and program procedures. He or she may misunderstand the forms and lose benefits as a consequence. Straightening out the resulting red tape may be impossible for a deaf person. Few service agencies, health centers, hospitals, or public libraries have either TDDs or staff who know sign language, and very few employ qualified sign language interpreters.

Applications of Section 504

If a deaf person seeks service from any federally funded agency and is turned away or otherwise discouraged because of communication barriers, that agency has violated Section 504.[1] If a job training program takes a deaf person's application but, because of the deafness, does not actively seek to place that person, it has violated the law. If an agency provides information or services by telephone but does not

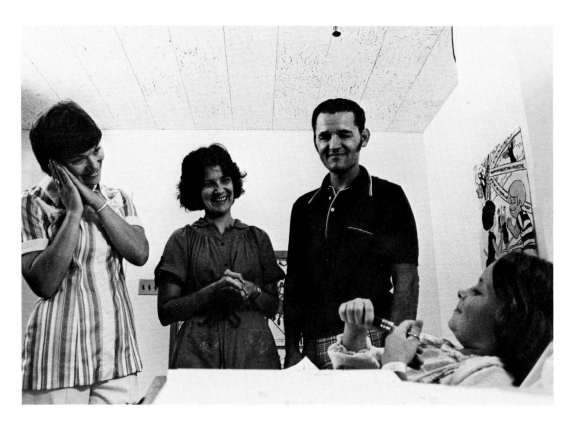

have a TDD or access to a TDD relay service, it has violated Section 504.[2]

Health, welfare, and social service agencies with fifteen or more employees must provide appropriate "auxiliary aids" to people with impaired sensory, manual, or speaking skills when necessary to afford such people an equal opportunity to benefit from the service in question.[3] Auxiliary aids are specifically defined to include braille, taped material, interpreters, and other aids.[4] Smaller agencies may also be required to provide auxiliary aids when doing so would not impair the agency's ability to provide its normal benefits or ser-

vices.[5] Interpreters can be hired for a reasonable hourly fee for occasional deaf clients. Many TDDs can be acquired for a one-time investment of a few hundred dollars. These expenses are not unduly burdensome for most agencies.

The section obligating social service agencies to ensure adequate communication with deaf people applies to many public and nonprofit agencies. For example, food stamp offices must provide an interpreter to assist in explaining the application procedure, eligibility criteria, and available benefits to deaf applicants. In addition, such offices must have a TDD so that deaf people can telephone for information, schedule appointments, or consult with caseworkers. New Jersey provided TDDs in all vocational rehabilitation offices that serve deaf clients.

While such an agency is not required to have an interpreter on staff at all times, deaf people should be able to request an interpreter if needed and to schedule an appointment when an interpreter is available. This appointment procedure is a reasonable method of providing equivalent services, even if applications are ordinarily handled on a first-come, first-served basis. The agency should also post a notice clearly explaining that interpreters are available and how to arrange an interpreted appointment.

Agency Responsibilities

Deaf people should be aware that many service agencies attempt to evade their legal responsibilities. Small agencies may try to do so by claiming that provision of auxiliary aids is beyond their financial means. They may, on the basis of their small size and budget, seek a waiver of the requirement that they provide aids. But some aids are critical for deaf people, and most of the essential aids are not excessive in cost. Deaf clients are entitled by law to aids they need. They should be provided free of charge to the deaf client. The cost is the responsibility of the agency receiving and making use of the federal money.

There are many ways an agency, health center, or hospital can make its services available and useful to deaf people. The Social Security Administration (SSA), for example, has announced a policy of providing interpreter services in all SSA proceedings and activities.* The SSA uses either an employee who is proficient in sign language or a professional sign language interpreter. No hearing-impaired person is required to use an interpreter with whom he or she is unable to communicate; the ultimate judge of an interpreter's competence is the deaf client.

The SSA has also installed a nationwide toll-free TDD. Operators at this number will relay calls to local SSA offices if necessary. The SSA also has installed TDD units in some local and regional offices. The decision to provide auxiliary aids shows wisdom and prudence. In the long run the aids will save money and staff time because communication will be effective and paperwork will be done correctly the first time.

Agency Rules and State Laws

In addition to the requirements of Section 504, most agencies have specific rules that prohibit discrimination against handicapped people in services

---

*See Appendix C for a Social Security Administration memorandum outlining procedures to be used by SSA personnel in securing interpreter services.

they support.[6] Some states have adopted laws that prohibit discrimination against handicapped people by government and private social service agencies. Others have laws specifically requiring certain services for deaf people. A New Mexico law requires state health, welfare, and educational agencies to provide interpreters whenever a deaf person seeks services or needs to communicate with agency personnel. Virginia has established a special agency, the Virginia Council for the Deaf, to provide interpreters to state departments and agencies, local govern-

ments, and any other organization or individual needing them. The government agencies are required to pay for the interpreters. A few states have laws that require installation of TDDs in hospitals and public agencies such as police stations.[7]

Most states have civil rights laws prohibiting discrimination by facilities open to the public. Traditionally, these laws have dealt only with racial or religious discrimination; more recently, some of them have been amended to prohibit discrimination based on handicap as well. In addition to commercial enterprises such as restaurants, hotels, and stores, these laws apply to service agencies that are open to the public.[8] A few states have adopted detailed laws mandating access and service for handicapped people. The Michigan Handicapper's Civil Rights Act, for example, guarantees a handicapped person full and equal utilization of public accommodations and services.

Hospital Communication Barriers

Before HEW's Section 504 regulations became effective in 1977, hearing-impaired people had virtually no right to effective communication in hospital care. When deaf people entered a hospital, they had to take what was offered them, sometimes settling for ineffective health care because they did not understand what was being said to them. Complicated medical terms were used with the hope that the deaf patient would understand them. Drugs were prescribed without any explanation of how to take them. Sometimes deaf people took these drugs with other medicines, not knowing the possible reactions. Hospital admissions procedures were rarely explained to them. If they wanted assistance from the nursing staff, they could not use the intercom to request specific kinds of services. If a pregnant woman went into the labor room, she could not bring an interpreter with her. She could not understand what her doctor wanted her to do, because the doctor's surgical mask made lipreading impossible.

A very important ingredient of health care is communication. Without communication, the patient cannot explain the symptoms of his or her illness to the medical staff. Without communication, the patient cannot comprehend the routines of preventive medicine. If all medical patients were treated like this, the general population would be outraged. Yet hearing-impaired people face these circumstances daily.

For the deaf person who has been deaf since birth (prelingually deaf), the English language is as comprehensible as a foreign language would be to an English-speaking person. The deaf person, having never heard English, has difficulty understanding.

The postlingually deaf person (deafened after the acquisition of language) has developed language, but he or she must compensate for that hearing loss by either matching words to lip movements or using sign language. Since lipreading is generally only 30 percent understandable, other means of communication must compensate for the remaining 70 percent. The postlingually deaf person usually can make use of signs, guesswork, or notes to grasp the remaining 70 percent.

Compounding the Stress

When a person is in a medical situation, he or she is sometimes apprehensive, nervous, confused, and in pain. When those feelings are compounded by the stress of trying to understand what a medical person is saying, the experience can be traumatic.

In the past, many hospitals have generally relied on the exchange of written notes, lipreading, or other less than satisfactory means to communicate with their deaf patients. For a deaf person with limited English skills, written English can be both ineffective and frustrating. Understanding is further hampered by unfamiliar medical terms and the need for fast, efficient communication during a medical emergency. Some hospitals attempt to get by with a staff member who has some knowledge of sign language, instead of bringing in a skilled interpreter from outside the hospital. This would be acceptable if the staff member were qualified, but this is rarely the case. More often the staff member's limited understanding of sign language creates serious misunderstandings, leading to ineffective treatment and even misdiagnosis.

Communication that is "effective"

and aids that are "appropriate"—two terms used in federal regulations—are best determined by the deaf patient. A series of complaints filed with HHS, however, demonstrates how hospital personnel often assume that they are better able than the deaf patient to decide how to communicate. In one case a hospital insisted that, since they could understand the deaf patient's voice, the patient could therefore understand them, despite the patient's repeated requests for an interpreter. In another case, a hospital stated that communication by means of pen and paper was adequate and that the decision to utilize an interpreter was up to the doctor. In a third case, a hospital arbitrarily stated that it would use a typewriter instead of an interpreter to communicate with a patient. In another case involving medical care for fourteen elderly deaf patients, a hospital claimed to have an interpreter on its staff. In fact, the interpreter had studied sign language for only one semester and could not read many of the deaf patients' signs.

The importance of using a qualified sign language interpreter cannot be overemphasized. A qualified interpreter has both the expressive and receptive skills to communicate effectively with a deaf person.

Clarifying the Regulations

In 1979 the National Center for Law and the Deaf (NCLD) filed complaints with the Office for Civil Rights (OCR) in Chicago. The complaints concerned interpretation of Section 504 regulations then in effect at HEW (see box on p. 61). Investigations of eight major hospitals were conducted. The investigations pointed out the need for further clarification of the regulations. A policy on the provision of auxiliary aids for hearing-impaired patients in inpatient, outpatient, and emergency treatment settings was released by OCR to its regional offices in May 1980. The policy states:

> The Department's Section 504 Regulation requires that health care providers be prepared to offer a full variety of communication options (auxiliary aids) in order to make sure that hearing-impaired persons are provided effective health care services. Those communication options are required to have been selected with consultation by "handicapped persons or organizations representing handicapped persons" in a self-evaluation which is done by the health care provider. This variety of options, which must be provided at no cost to the hearing-impaired patient, must include:
> - formal arrangements with interpreters who can accurately and fluently express and receive in sign language;
> - supplemental hearing devices such as amplified telephone and loop systems for meetings;
> - written communication;
> - flash cards and staff training in basic sign language expressions related to emergency treatment.
> The names, addresses, phone numbers, and hours of availability of

The HHS Section 504 regulations and guidelines seek to address the unique problems facing deaf health care patients. The regulations state:

a. General. In providing health, welfare, or other social services or benefits, a recipient may not, on the basis of handicap:

1. Deny a qualified handicapped person these benefits or services;
2. Afford a qualified handicapped person an opportunity to receive benefits or services that are not equal to that offered nonhandicapped persons;
3. Provide a qualified handicapped person with benefits or services that are not as effective (as defined in § 84.4[b]) as those provided to others;
4. Provide benefits or services in a manner that limits or has the effect of limiting the participation of qualified handicapped persons; or
5. Provide different or separate benefits or services to handicapped persons except where necessary to provide qualified handicapped persons with benefits and services that are as effective as those provided to others.

b. Notice. A recipient that provides notice concerning benefits or services or written material concerning waivers of rights or consent to treatment shall take such steps as are necessary to ensure that qualified handicapped persons, including those with impaired sensory or speaking skills, are not denied effective notice.

c. Emergency treatment of the hearing-impaired. A recipient hospital that provides health services or benefits shall establish a procedure for effective communication with persons with impaired hearing for the purpose of providing emergency health care.

d. Auxiliary aids.

1. A recipient to which this subpart applies that employs fifteen or more persons shall provide appropriate auxiliary aids to persons with impaired sensory, manual, or speaking skills, where necessary to afford such persons an equal opportunity to benefit from the service in question.
2. The Director may require recipients with fewer than fifteen employees to provide auxiliary aids where the provision of aids would not significantly impair the ability of the recipient to provide its benefits or services.
3. For the purpose of this paragraph, auxiliary aids may include brailled and taped materials, interpreters, and other aids.[9]

interpreters must be available to the health provider's employees. Health care providers have a responsibility to make sure that hearing-impaired persons seeking treatment are given advance notice of the various communication options. Family members may be used only if they are specifically requested by the hearing-impaired person. In addition, health care providers must have at least one teletypewriter (TDD/TTY) or an arrangement to share a TTY line with other health facilities.

In most circumstances, the deaf person is in the best position to judge which means of communication will give him/her equal opportunity in health service. The patient's judgment in choosing effective communication must be considered of utmost importance. If there is any disagreement between the health care provider and the hearing-impaired person regarding communication needs, the usual practice is to respect the hearing-impaired person's judgment. The risks are greater when there is inaccurate or incomplete communication than when the health care staff have little or no information on the patient's medical history or specific health care needs. Wrong diagnosis can be made, wrong medicine can be given, or an operation can be performed for the wrong reasons if inaccurate or incomplete information is given.

But, in emergency health care, it may not always be possible to provide a specific kind of communication for a hearing-impaired person. Health care facilities must, however, provide the most effective communication in view of the limits of time in the emergency situation.[10]

Emergency Care

The emergency health care regulations are especially important. Hospitals are required to establish a special emergency health care procedure for "effective communication" with deaf and hearing-impaired people in emergency rooms.[11] The hospitals should be able to locate qualified sign language interpreters on very short notice. They should also have TDD-equipped telephones, so that a deaf person can alert the hospital that a deaf patient is coming in and will need an interpreter or other special services. The TDD equipment also will permit the hospitalized deaf person to make calls to family or medical personnel. Emergency room staff can be trained to use and recognize basic sign language necessary for emergency care. In addition they should be trained to recognize quickly that a person is hearing

impaired and to know how to find appropriate auxiliary aids.

Hospital Compliance

The following examples show how a hospital or health center may accommodate deaf patients and comply with other sections of the regulations. A hospital that ordinarily allows only one person to accompany a woman through natural childbirth may have to alter its delivery room rules to allow both the husband and an interpreter to be present during the delivery. A hospital that prohibits admission of deaf people to its psychiatric unit unless they read lips will have to change its policy to comply with Section 504 regulations. Services must be equivalent.

When a patient is in a hospital room, there are many devices that he or she can depend on to make the hospital stay easier. For the deaf patient, many of these devices are useless and might just as well not exist. For example, if a deaf patient presses the intercom button, the nurse at the station will answer—but they cannot communicate. After repeated attempts to contact each other, the nurse and the deaf patient may become exasperated with each other. The deaf patient assumes the nurse knows that he or she is deaf, not realizing that the nurse just came on duty and "forgot" there was a deaf patient in Room 121. The nurse may think that the patient is hitting the button by accident and decide to ignore the buzzing intercom. This typical problem can be prevented by "flagging" deaf patients' charts and intercom buttons so that all pertinent hospital personnel are aware of the special situation.

Hospitals must also provide ongoing staff training to sensitize personnel to other special needs of hearing-impaired people: adequate, glare-free lighting; control of background noise for all hearing-aid wearers; modifications to auditory fire alarm systems; changes in oral evaluation procedures; and freeing a patient's hands and arms for signing and gesturing.

Health care facilities should take special steps to make sure that deaf and blind people know about services the hospital normally offers and about any special services to which they may be entitled because of their disabilities. For example, many hospitals provide new patients some kind of orientation to the hospital and its personnel and services. All such information should be available in writing at an English level that most people can understand. It should include an easy-to-read notice about the availability of sign language interpreters, portable TDDs, and other special services for disabled people.

If a facility gives information about its services by telephone, it should ensure that deaf people can get the same information using a TDD-equipped telephone. Hospitals also should have easy-to-read notices posted in the emergency room, outpatient clinic, and all admitting areas which inform deaf people of sign language interpreter services or other assistance and how to get them. Few deaf people realize that such services are available or know how to request them. It is the hospital's responsibility to provide this information.

Hospitals often ask patients to sign a written consent to treatment or legal waivers of rights before they will treat them. Section 504 requires hospitals to take any necessary steps so that deaf and blind people understand these rights. A deaf patient should ask the hospital to have the consent papers explained in sign language. The consent and waiver papers also should be written in language that is easy for the deaf patient to understand.

Guidelines for Hospitals

The following guidelines were written by NCLD to help hospital administrators develop procedures for serving the needs of their deaf patients and comply with Section 504 regulations:

- A central office should be designated to supervise services to deaf patients. This office should establish a system to obtain qualified sign language and oral interpreters on short notice twenty-four hours a day.

- The unit to which a deaf patient is admitted should immediately notify the designated office when a deaf patient is admitted.

- An interpreter, if available within the hospital, should be sent to the patient immediately to consult with the patient as to the appropriate method of communication, which may include:

  —Use of a qualified sign language and/or oral interpreter;
  —Lipreading;
  —Handwritten notes;
  —Supplemental hearing devices, or any combination of the above.

The interpreter should give the patient notice of the right to a qualified sign language and/or oral interpreter to be provided by the hospital without charge to the patient. If no interpreter is available within the hospital, the patient should be given written notice of these rights.

- The interpreter assists in communication between the patient and the staff in all situations

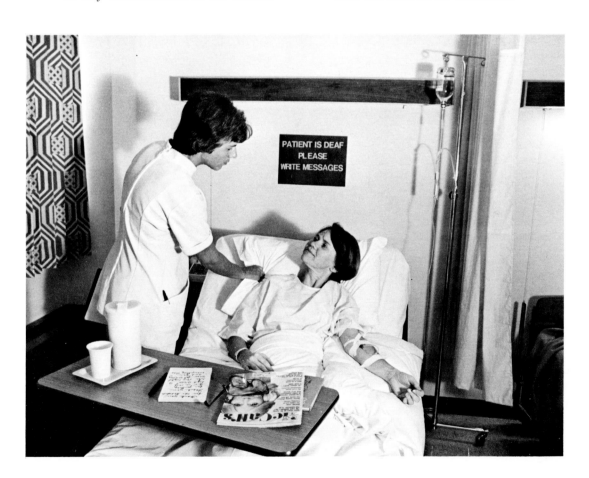

where effective communication is necessary to ensure that the deaf patient is receiving equal services and equal opportunity to participate in and to benefit from hospital services. These situations include but are not limited to:

—Obtaining the patient's medical history;

—Obtaining informed consent or permission for treatment;

—Diagnosis of the ailment or injury;

—Explanations of medical procedures to be used;

—Treatment or surgery if the patient is conscious, or to determine if the patient is conscious;

—Those times the patient is in intensive care or in the recovery room after surgery;

—Emergency situations that arise;

—Explanations of the medications prescribed, how and when they are to be taken, and possible side effects;

—Assisting at the request of the doctor or other hospital staff; and

—Discharge of the patient.

Friends or relatives of a deaf patient

should not be used as interpreters unless the deaf patient specifically requests that they interpret. Deaf patients, their friends, and their families should be told that a professional interpreter will be engaged where needed for effective communication.

- The deaf patient should be informed that another interpreter will be obtained if the patient is unable to communicate with a particular interpreter.

- Any written notices of rights or services and written consent forms should be written at no higher than a fifth-grade reading level. An interpreter should be provided if the deaf patient is unable to understand such written notices.

- A telecommunications device for the deaf (TDD) should be obtained and used for making appointments, giving out information, and assisting in emergency situations. Portable TDDs should be available on request for deaf inpatients. Telephone amplifiers should be provided for hearing-impaired patients. All telephones should be compatible with hearing aids equipped with a telephone switch.

- Alternative methods to auditory intercom systems, paging systems, and alarm systems should be provided for all hearing-impaired patients.

- Ongoing efforts should be made by the hospital to sensitize staff to the various special needs of deaf patients.

- Contact with local deaf people, organizations for and of the deaf, and the community agencies serving deaf people should be maintained for assistance in drawing up a list of qualified interpreters and in developing a program of hospital services that is responsive to the needs of deaf patients.

Direct Care Staff

Hospital staff can do many things to enable communication with a deaf patient, to make the patient more comfortable with the hospital environment, and thereby to serve the patient better. Common sense and basic information about deafness will help hospital staff to provide good health care.

The deaf patient is the best resource regarding the preferred mode of communication and should be consulted about this and about any problems that arise. The isolation of deaf people can be overcome to a great extent by explaining what is happening and answering any questions the patient might have.

The importance of using a qualified interpreter to ensure effective communication cannot be overemphasized. However, there may be many routine situations—such as bringing dinner or taking temperature—where an interpreter is not necessary. The following guidelines on working with deaf patients will help compensate for the absence of an interpreter. These guidelines, if implemented, will also improve the quality of care provided.

Make added efforts in communication to ensure that the patient understands what is happening.

- Allow more time for every communication, not rushing through what is said. To make sure the patient understands, some thoughts should be repeated using different phrases.

- Lip movements should not be exaggerated. Speak at a normal rate of speed and separate words.

- Patient's arms should not be restricted; they should be free to write and sign.

- Make cards or posters of usual questions and responses that can be pointed to quickly.

- Keep paper and pen handy, but be sensitive to the patient's level of English language fluency and writing skills.

Be sensitive to the visual environment of deaf patients by adjusting lighting and using visual rather than auditory cues and reassurances.

- Use charts, pictures, and/or three-dimensional models when explaining information and procedures to deaf patients.

- Do not remove a deaf patient's glasses or leave a deaf patient in total darkness.

- Remove any bright lights in front of the deaf person when communicating; glare makes it difficult to read signs or lips.

- Face the patient when speaking, without covering your face or mouth.

- Keep facial expressions pleasant and unworried so as not to alarm the patient.

Alert all staff to the presence and needs of the deaf patient and be sensitive to those needs.

- "Flag" the intercom button so that workers will know the patient is deaf and requires a personal visit rather than a response over the intercom.
- "Flag" the patient's charts, room, and bed to alert staff to use appropriate means of communication.

Sensitivity to the special needs of people with hearing aids requires that hospital personnel:

- Allow the patient to wear the hearing aid.
- Don't shout at the patient.

- Be sure that the patient has fully understood what is said.

Training Models

Many health care providers wonder what kind of training will best prepare their staffs to meet the needs of hearing-impaired people. Specialized training is both very important and very hard to find. Not enough attention has been paid to the needs of hearing-impaired people, let alone to ways of meeting those needs. Deafness and hearing impairment are largely silent—

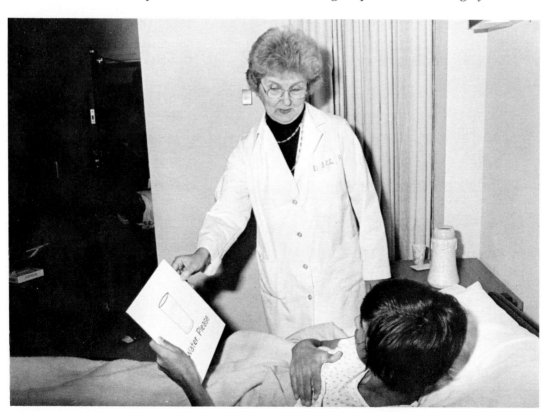

and therefore often neglected—handicaps. They are the most common disabilities in the U.S. today, and they are the most misunderstood. To help overcome this misunderstanding, two kinds of training for health care providers are now being conducted.

The first is a model training concept. The National Academy at Gallaudet College has developed a training packet for nurses on how to care for deaf patients. The packet has been given to a variety of hospitals across the country and features training films, slides, and lectures. The nurses learn how to approach their deaf patients and how to understand the individuality of each patient. This one-session training seminar is a model project designed to initiate continuous seminars. Nurses are encouraged to keep up their training, and their hospitals are encouraged to keep in touch with the National Academy for further training materials and instructions.[12]

The second kind of training is local effort to educate health care providers and the deaf community. A two-way educational process in maternal and childcare health is being undertaken at the community level by Deafpride of Washington, D.C. The project was established after the mother of a young deaf child saw the problems deaf mothers had in getting medical care. The project prepares deaf women for delivery and maternal care by holding "rap sessions." It conducts workshops for both health care providers and the

hearing-impaired patient. The project has TDDs at two community health clinics plus ongoing services at Howard University Hospital in the District of Columbia and Prince George's General Hospital in nearby Maryland.[13]

These educational programs have produced a growing awareness among both medical providers and hearing-impaired consumers about the importance of ongoing education about Section 504.

For deaf people to receive effective hospital care, hospital administrators must be informed of their Section 504 obligations. Hospital personnel need to be educated and trained to meet the special needs of deaf patients. The general community needs to understand how important it is to provide quality medical care for the deaf community. And the deaf patient needs to understand his or her rights.

Notes

1. 45 *Code of Federal Regulations* §84.52(a)

2. 45 C.F.R. §84.21(f)

3. 45 C.F.R. §84.52(d)(1)

4. 45 C.F.R. §84.52(d)(3)

5. 45 C.F.R. §84.52(d)(2)

6. In the HHS Section 504 regulation, these rules are in Subpart F, 45 C.F.R. §84.51 *et seq.* The Office of Revenue Sharing—pursuant to Section 122(a) of the State and Local Assistance Act of 1972, as amended in 31 *United States Code* §1242(a)—has invoked the HHS Section 504 regulation for recipient state and local governments.

7. E.g., see Washington Rev. Code §70-54.

8. Maryland Human Relations Code Ann. §498; Maine Rev. Stat. Tit. 5 §4591.

9. 45 C.F.R. §84.52

10. "Position on the Provision of Auxiliary Aids for Hearing-Impaired Patients in Inpatient, Outpatient, and Emergency Treatment Settings," memorandum from Roma J. Stewart (Director, Office for Civil Rights, Department of Health, Education, and Welfare) to regional directors, April 21, 1980.

11. 45 C.F.R. §84.52(c)

12. The National Academy, Gallaudet College, Kendall Green, Washington, DC 20002.

13. Deafpride, Inc., 2010 Rhode Island Ave. NE, Washington, DC 20018.

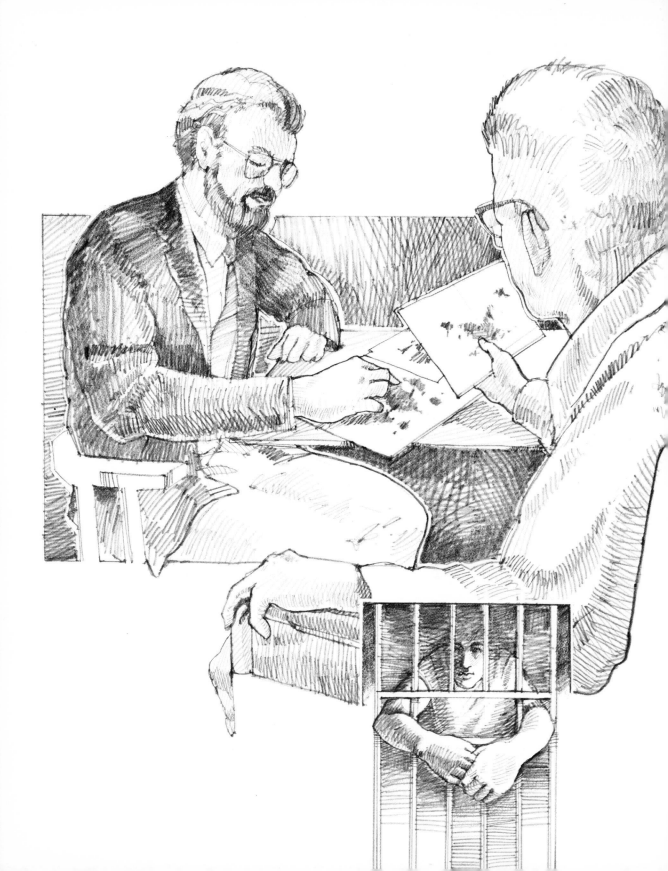

CHAPTER SIX
Mental Health

An attendant stands in the middle of the mental health unit shouting at a patient. For thirty-five years the hospital attendants have tried to communicate by yelling at him. They still do not know that he is deaf.

This man and his situation are real. He is like many deaf people in mental health facilities who suffer from misdiagnosis or maltreatment. At the same time, the needs of many other deaf people for mental health care go unmet.

Approximately 43,000 or 10 percent of the prevocationally deaf population need mental health services, but fewer than 2 percent receive them.[1] Progressive programs exist in some states and the District of Columbia, but there are few mental health facilities functioning specifically for deaf patients. Also, few regular facilities are even modestly staffed and equipped to help deaf patients, in spite of the relative ease and minimal expense with which the patients can be aided.

The primary problem is the lack of competent mental health professionals who have skill in communicating with and understanding deaf people. Even with an interpreter present, the mental health professional must be empathetic to deaf people and their culture if therapy is to be effective.

The direct and frequent result of miscommunication is misinterpretation of the patient's deafness and speechlessness as psychopathology or retardation. A misdiagnosis usually results in improper placement, misguided treatment and case management, unjustified exclusion of the patient from hospital programs and activities, and inappropriate aftercare. The sad result is the patient's isolation, bewilderment, and even rage, all of which run counter to the purposes of the facility and its staff.

This chapter is adapted from S. DuBow, "Legal Strategies to Improve Mental Health Care for Deaf People." In L. K. Stein, E. D. Mindel, and T. J. Jabaley, eds., *Deafness and Mental Health* (New York: Grune & Stratton, 1981), pp. 195–210. Used by permission of the publisher.

A survey of New York state psychiatric hospitals revealed that more than one-fourth of their deaf patients had been diagnosed as mentally deficient, as contrasted with only 3.7 percent of the nondeaf.[2] McCay Vernon, a psychologist noted for his work with deaf people, observes:

> It has been established that IQ is essentially normally distributed in the deaf population. Obviously gross error had been made in the fundamental but relatively easy-to-make diagnosis of mental retardation.[3]

A study of Illinois state mental hospitals found that staff in three-quarters of the facilities had no concept of which patients were deaf. One hospital with approximately 4,000 patients provided the names of 200 patients considered to be deaf; only one of them was actually deaf. On the other hand, five deaf patients, none of whose names was on the list, were found in just one unit. Many of the deaf patients thought they were the only deaf people in the hospital. The authors of the study noted:

> Obviously, if the deaf patients were not even identified as deaf, no real effort was made to treat them. No staff members or other patients could communicate with them in the language of signs. Thus, they were total isolates. In fact, in this sense, their hospitalization was actually anti-therapeutic.[4]

Misdiagnosis can result in the deaf patient being inappropriately assigned and confined to an institution for many years before the mistake is discovered.

There are numerous accounts of misdiagnosis similar to that which opened this chapter. Vernon, for example, reported the case of a patient who spent thirty-five years at Idaho's state school and hospital for the mentally retarded when deafness was the patient's primary disability.

Donald Lang

A celebrated and often cited criminal case illustrates how misdiagnosis and an absence of appropriate services can affect a deaf person's life.

Donald Lang of Chicago is unable to hear, speak, read, or write. He has been accused of two gruesome rape-murders and, for more than fifteen years, has been confined to mental hospitals and jails. For equally long, Illinois courts, lawyers, and mental health officials have struggled to decide what to do with him.

When Lang was first accused of murder in 1966, he was found to be mentally and physically incompetent to stand trial, and he was committed to a mental hospital for life. Lang appealed, and the state supreme court ruled that Lang should be given a trial to determine his guilt and, if found not guilty, released.[5] By the time of the trial, however, one of the state's principal witnesses had died. The charge was dropped, and Lang was released in 1970.

In 1972, he was again charged with a similar rape-murder. Citing the Illinois Supreme Court's decision in his first

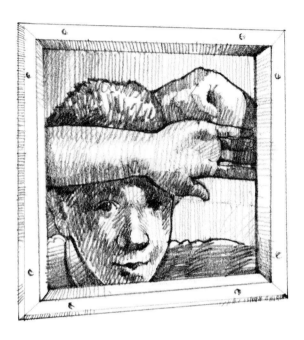

criticized the state's attorney's office, the mental health department, and the Illinois legislature because of the desperate need for rehabilitation capability and for change in Illinois' law and practice.

In Illinois, contrary to the laws of some other states, the courts do not have the power to take defendants unfit to stand trial and commit them to mental health departments for proper treatment. Without such changes in Illinois, Lang cannot get treatment until he is exonerated, but he cannot be exonerated until he gets treatment.

Theon Jackson

A case similar to Donald Lang's was decided by the U.S. Supreme Court.[8] Theon Jackson, an illiterate, mentally retarded deaf person with no basic communication skills, was accused of purse snatching. An Indiana court committed Jackson to a mental institution due to his inability to understand the nature of the charges against him. His commitment was to continue until his sanity could be certified to the court.

The Supreme Court reversed the state court decision, declaring that Jackson's constitutional rights were violated since he was condemned to permanent institutionalization without the necessary showing required for commitment under the state statute. If it could not justify continued confinement after six months, the state was ordered to proceed to trial or dismiss the case.

Both of these cases raise the issues of

case, Lang chose to stand trial and was convicted. The state supreme court reversed the conviction, ruling that the trial was constitutionally impermissible because it had been conducted without aids which would have allowed Lang to understand the nature and object of the proceedings against him, consult with his attorney, and assist in preparing his defense.[6]

The Illinois Appellate Court ruled in June 1978 that, because Lang was neither mentally ill nor retarded, the department of mental health did not have to develop a training program to make Lang fit for trial.[7] At the same time, it

a deaf person's fitness to stand trial for a criminal offense and the applicable standard for commitment. Both Lang and Jackson were found incompetent to stand trial. The traditional test for competence is whether the defendant understands the proceedings and charges and whether he or she can consult with a lawyer and assist actively in presenting the defense.[9]

Lang and Jackson were found incompetent to stand trial, but this stemmed from an inability to communicate, not from mental illness. A finding of incompetence usually results in commitment to a mental health facility until such time as the individual becomes competent. Yet restoration of competence for Lang and Jackson was highly unlikely. In the Jackson case, the Supreme Court realized that the result of this procedure—permanent institutionalization—violates the constitutional rights of the defendant.

To remedy this inequity, the Supreme Court held that any incompetency commitment must be temporary and reasonably likely to be effective in restoring the defendant to competency. If there is no substantial probability that the defendant's condition is treatable, commitment either is not allowed or must be terminated if it has already taken place. The Court thus attacked

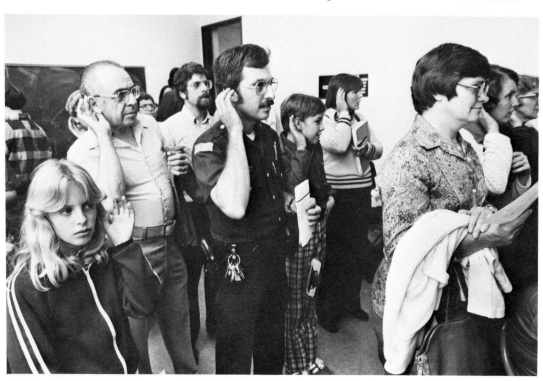

the rigid interpretation of competency and commitment standards applied by the state that resulted in the deprivation of Jackson's constitutional rights.

Presumably, the law that has developed as a result of these two cases would prevent deaf people accused of crimes from being institutionalized without proper treatment and without hope of being tried for the crime charged. Yet, practical problems remain in the implementation of these two judicial decisions. The Lang case demonstrates the problems in developing programs to train "incompetent" individuals to improve their communication skills and participate in their criminal defense. Who is responsible for developing these programs and what they will consist of remain unanswered questions. And although the Indiana court spoke of committing Jackson for a reasonable time until competency is restored, no guidelines were provided as to how long a reasonable period of time is.

These practical problems seriously impair any protections guaranteed by the cases of Lang and Jackson. Until judicial decisions or legislation further clarify these issues and find solutions for these problems, deaf defendants, adjudged incompetent to stand trial, will continue to suffer the loss of their constitutional rights.

Programs for Deaf People

Another dismaying problem that affects deaf and deaf-blind patients is the abuse sometimes inflicted on them. Unable to summon help or to identify attackers, they and their food and property are easy targets for more aggressive patients. Even in well-managed facilities, where these abuses are rare, the deaf person may find the very process of institutionalization brutal to the psyche, because he or she can understand little or nothing of what is happening in the place.

Responding to the problems, some hospitals and mental health administrations in the states and the District of Columbia have begun to develop specific programs for deaf people.[10] Examples are Saint Elizabeths Hospital in Washington, D.C., and new programs in Michigan and Maryland.

Deaf people, their hearing advocates, and the state government combined efforts in Michigan to establish a Center for Deaf Treatment Services (CDTS). Under the state department of mental health, the pilot program includes a twenty-bed inpatient unit to serve hearing-impaired persons over the age of seventeen. The philosophy behind the treatment approach is that the psychological consequences of deafness are primarily responsible for the problems in these patients' personality development. The approach is a key which opens new possibilities for intervention and treatment. Patients in the deaf unit are taught sign language, which is used in all individual and group therapy.

In addition to inpatient services, CDTS staff is available to provide education, consultation, diagnostic, and evaluation services to other institutions and community mental health programs. The center plans to set up several outpatient clinics throughout the state.

Some states fund deaf units through their departments of mental health; other states channel such funding to departments of vocational rehabilitation. Some deaf units have a mix of federal and state grants to pursue their work; because such grants are temporary, though, new ones must be sought constantly.

When no leadership exists in a state mental health system or vocational rehabilitation department, or when the legislature is indifferent, then alternate points of initiating change must be found. Courts are increasingly recognizing that mental patients have legal rights, so legal action may serve to improve mental health services for deaf patients.

Legal Action

Legal action can be on behalf of an individual or a class of people. In the first, a single person seeks relief from a situation. In the second, a person who claims to represent all people similarly situated brings a suit on their behalf. Each method has been used to achieve some impressive victories.

There are two kinds of individual action: a civil damage suit and a writ of habeas corpus. A civil damage suit

is used when a patient sues physicians who neglect his or her care. A famous case of this type involved Kenneth Donaldson, who was committed to a Florida state mental hospital for fifteen years without receiving treatment. In the landmark case, *O'Connor v. Donaldson*, the U.S. Supreme Court held that it is unconstitutional to confine against their wills nondangerous people who are capable of living outside the institution and who are not receiving treatment.[11]

The second kind of individual action is the writ of habeas corpus, a traditional tool for challenging conditions of confinement, whether in jail or some other institution. It is the most appropriate legal method for patients who have been misdiagnosed or committed because proper placements were not available. It can be used to challenge overly restrictive conditions or inappropriate treatment and to obtain services or placements that are more fitting.

Habeas corpus was successfully used in the District of Columbia to challenge placement of patients in excessively restrictive treatment settings. According to District of Columbia statutes, the purpose of involuntary commitment is treatment; confinement may legally restrict liberty only insofar as it is necessary to treat the patient. For example, a patient with a mild disorder cannot be locked in a maximum security ward used to house the criminally insane. Patients have a right to the form of treatment which is least restrictive.[12]

Some courts have even held that a hospital has an obligation to explore alternative placements for each of its patients and to select that placement which is least restrictive.[13]

One problem with habeas corpus is the standard used in judging whether the hospital has acted improperly. The court does not require that the hospital make the best choice of treatments but only that it make a permissible and reasonable choice in light of the relevant information it possesses.[14] It is difficult, therefore, for the patient to prove that the hospital has acted unreasonably or improperly in choosing treatment. The habeas corpus process is also expensive and time-consuming. Cases are often difficult because they are litigated individually. Also, while the case is in progress, the hospital can reassign the patient or change the terms of confinement. The court can then dismiss the patient's claim of inadequate treatment because the patient's status, even if not improved, has changed.

Class Action Suits

Because of the difficulty in bringing individual suits and the limitation of the remedy only to the patient who brought the suit, class action has proved to be a more effective means of achieving institutional change. A class action suit is filed by a patient who claims to represent all people similarly situated. Because the remedy resulting from the action applies to all such people, class action litigation often results in the definition and articulation of rights of mental patients, minimum standards for care and treatment, and responsibilities and liabilities of the treating staff.

A famous class action suit, *Wyatt v. Stickney*, later called *Wyatt v. Aderholt*, resulted in the recognition and establishment of a mental patient's constitutional right to be treated and not merely held in custodial care.[15]

The court issued a far-reaching and effective decision, ruling specifically that patients involuntarily committed through noncriminal procedures to a state mental hospital have a constitutional right to receive such individual treatment as will give them an opportunity to improve their mental condition or be cured. The court decreed minimal constitutional standards for adequate treatment, including an individual treatment plan that provides a statement of the least restrictive treatment conditions necessary to achieve the purposes of commitment. Other rights were specifically recognized: the rights to a humane psychological and physical environment, privacy, dignity, and freedom from isolation. The court also established a human rights committee to investigate violations of patients' rights and to oversee implementation of the plan. It also ordered a minimum number of treatment personnel per 250 patients and other changes to ensure more humane living conditions.

The effects of this decision for deaf people are potentially great, because

ing training in sign language, the program would allow the patient to participate fully in therapy and to interact with staff and other deaf patients, who themselves would know or be learning sign language. The emphasis on communication skills would be a central aspect of therapy and rehabilitation, allowing the patient the opportunity for social adjustment and eventual integration into society.

Another effective legal strategy based on constitutional law is use of the "protection from harm" theory. The principle here is that confinement by the state should not cause a person's condition to deteriorate. This principle was successfully invoked to correct overcrowded conditions in New York's Willowbrook State School.[16] The court ruled that patients of a state institution have a right to protection from such inhumane treatment as would constitute cruel and unusual punishment under the eighth amendment. The ruling stated that treatment is impermissibly harmful not only when there is physical harm or deterioration but also when conditions that exist frustrate the full development of one's capabilities.

State Statutes

State law is often an effective basis for suit. Many states now have statutes guaranteeing a right to treatment in their institutions, a trend that began because of a highly influential legal decision in the District of Columbia, *Rouse v. Cameron.*[17] Filing a petition for ha-

current laws do not ensure that a deaf person will receive anything more than an interpreter—an accommodation that most professionals providing mental health care to deaf people agree is insufficient. The one-to-one relationship between the therapist and the patient is critical in therapy. However, under the *Wyatt* decision, an individualized treatment plan for a deaf person would probably include programs such as Michigan's Center for Deaf Treatment Services (described earlier). By includ-

beas corpus, the patient relied on a District law to contend that he had a right to be treated, not merely confined. The law states:

> A person hospitalized in a public hospital for a mental illness shall, during his hospitalization, be entitled to medical and psychiatric care and treatment. The administrator of each public hospital shall keep records detailing all medical and psychiatric care and treatment received by a person hospitalized for a mental illness. . . .[18]

The court construed this statute as granting the patient's contention, and other state courts have ruled similarly in interpreting their laws. One advantage of this approach is that judges in state courts will probably be more inclined to enforce state laws than to declare new constitutional rights.

In the last twenty years there has been substantial movement away from treatment in large institutions and toward treatment in the community. State reforms of their commitment procedures and policies, recent court decisions setting minimum standards for patient care, a new federal emphasis on community-based care, and the demand for appropriate treatment have all accelerated the movement toward provision of mental health services in the community.[19] By 1975 three out of every four people receiving mental health care did so as outpatients, primarily in community-based settings.[20]

Another influential ruling is *Dixon v. Weinberger*.[21] A federal court for the District of Columbia held that patients in Saint Elizabeths Hospital—a federally administered mental hospital and community mental health center in Washington, D.C.—have a right to treatment that specifically includes the right to be placed in facilities outside the institution once the institution determines that such a placement is appropriate. The court ruled that the United States and District of Columbia violated the District's 1964 Hospitalization of the Mentally Ill Act when they failed to place in alternative, less restrictive facilities those St. Elizabeths inpatients determined to be suitable for community placement. Less restrictive alternatives included nursing homes, foster homes, personal care homes, and halfway houses.

Right to Habilitation

Another important case involved the state of Maine.[22] A federal district court in Maine approved a consent decree that established detailed standards for the care and treatment of mentally retarded people who are placed in community settings. In the consent decree, Maine recognized that, regardless of their age and degree of retardation or other disability, people released from institutions into the community have the right to receive "habilitation." Habilitation specifically includes the right to an individualized plan of care, education, and training and to services including physical therapy, psychotherapy, speech therapy, and medical and dental attention.

The consent agreement was the first one that obligated a state to consider specifically what was required of it so that deaf people could benefit from the service it provides: (1) hearing-impaired outpatients who could not acquire speech would be taught sign language; (2) the state would provide sign language training to staff and other persons working with deaf citizens; (3) screenings for hearing ability would be conducted with each patient; (4) treatment and/or further evaluation would be provided by qualified speech and hearing professionals; and (5) hearing aids when needed would be provided and maintained in good working order. The court appointed a master to monitor implementation of the consent agreement.

The rights of mentally retarded persons were more narrowly defined, however, in a 1981 U.S. Supreme Court decision. In the case of *Pennhurst v. Halderman*,[23] the Court held that the Developmentally Disabled Assistance and Bill of Rights Act[24] does not necessarily require states to provide treatment in community settings to mentally retarded persons. The act's bill of rights states that mentally retarded individuals have the "right to appropriate treatment, services, and habilitation" in a "setting that is least restrictive of . . . personal liberty."[25] The Court held that Congress did not intend by this language to impose massive financial obligations on states.

The Court stated that Congress must make clear to the states any obligations to be imposed upon them through the receipt of federal financial assistance. This ruling reversed a lower court decision which held that the rights of mentally retarded residents of Pennhurst State School and Hospital were violated because of unsanitary, inhumane, and dangerous living conditions.

Consciousness Raising

Any future judicial construction of a right to community treatment for mental illness will have far-reaching influence on improving the noninstitutional care of deaf people. But at present, communication and attitudinal barriers, and the lack of qualified, capable staff, prevent most existing community facilities from satisfactorily meeting the mental health needs of their deaf clients. For deaf people to be released from institutions where they receive merely custodial care is no solution if all they can look forward to is inaccessible community services.

In terms of changing the way things are done, the involvement of the mental health profession will be more important than even future litigation. The profession must produce specific and practical solutions to the problems of people put into its care, and this includes deaf people. More and better training opportunities in deaf psychology, research, information dissemination, and cultural awareness are needed within the profession. The raising of consciousness should occur at every level.

State Legislation

From the point of view of increasing the number and quality of good laws and achieving effective levels of resource allocation, work with the state legislatures is absolutely necessary.* Good laws have as far reaching an impact as legal victories. Concerned people and organizations—mental health professionals, state mental health and vocational rehabilitation administrators, legislators, jurists, and disabled advocates and activists—ought to be natural allies in the effort to produce solutions that are effective, sensible, and not merely cosmetic.

Several states have set the pace. Georgia, Illinois, Massachusetts, Michigan, and Pennsylvania have recently changed their mental health laws to require individualized treatment plans.

The Georgia legislature amended its mental health law in order to elaborate the rights of patients in state mental health facilities.[26] These include the right to refuse treatment, the right to the least restrictive alternative for every patient, the right to placement in non-institutional community facilities and

_____
*See Chapter Twelve for more information on state legislatures and state commissions. The details of how one state legislature was persuaded to establish an outpatient mental health program for deaf people is recounted in that chapter.

programs as appropriate, and recourse to an established complaint procedure.

A 1977 amendment to the Illinois Mental Health Code specifically mandated individual treatment plans and use of sign language with any hearing-impaired patient for whom sign language is a primary mode of communication. Unfortunately, this amendment was excluded from a comprehensive reform of Illinois' mental health law in 1978; it remains a good model, though, for states to guarantee accessibility of mental health services to deaf people.[27]

Massachusetts' Mental Health Code requires that the cases of institutionalized patients receive periodic administrative review. An institution is required to determine a patient's relationship to his or her community and family, employment possibilties, and the availability of community resources in considering every possible alternative to continued hospitalization or care in a residential treatment center.[28]

Pennsylvania's 1976 Mental Health Resources Act requires institutions to develop an individualized plan for treatment of the patient's specific problem in the least restrictive environment. Treatment ranges from full-time inpatient care to partial hospitalization to outpatient care.[29]

The Georgia, Massachusetts, and Pennsylvania laws are good models because of their least-restrictive-environment requirements. Deaf people should be able to receive the entire range of housing and treatment

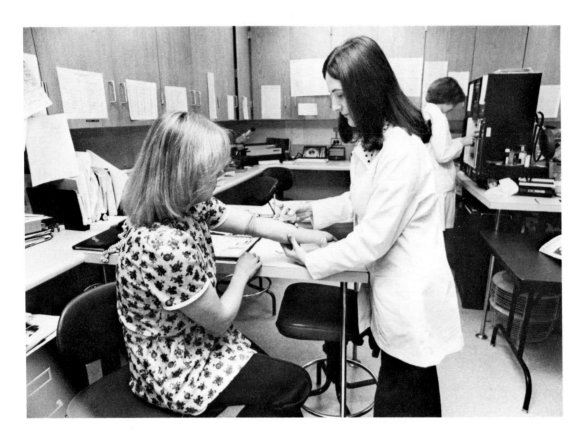

environments: community mental
health centers, nursing homes, personal
care homes, foster homes, and halfway
houses.

Advocacy Agencies

The enactment of progressive laws
and the creation of special programs
are milestones in the effort to assure
accessible and effective mental health
care for deaf people. To get other states
to change their laws and to fund necessary services will require perseverance,
coordination, and follow-through from
legislative activists. In states that have

not addressed the needs of their deaf
citizens, federal statutes are about the
only effective way to achieve even the
bare minimum of accommodation—the
means to communicate.

It is most important, for example,
that states enact laws providing independent advocacy agencies to protect
the civil rights of mental patients. Congress has required the creation of these
agencies in states that receive formula
grants under the Developmentally Disabled Assistance and Bill of Rights Act.
Specifically, the agencies have authority to "pursue legal, administrative, and

other appropriate remedies" in the protection of and advocacy for the rights of people receiving the state service. The agencies are required to be independent of the state entities that provide treatment, service, or habilitation to people with developmental disabilities.

Federal Regulations

Section 504 of the 1973 Rehabilitation Act is another statute with significant impact on the states. The federal regulations to this law require mental health facilities receiving Department of Health and Human Services' funding to provide effective benefits or services in a manner that does not limit or have the effect of limiting the participation of qualified handicapped people in the program. A recipient mental health agency or facility

> that employs fifteen or more persons shall provide appropriate auxiliary aids to persons with impaired sensory, manual, or speaking skills, where necessary to afford such persons an equal opportunity to benefit from the service in question. . . . For the purpose of this paragraph, auxiliary aids may include brailled and taped material, interpreters, and other aids for persons with impaired hearing or vision.[30]

Mental health service providers thus bear the responsibility of providing interpreters to deaf patients. Facilities that refuse to provide them risk a withholding or cutting off of their HHS funds or a private lawsuit against them. Several successful suits have been brought against universities, social service agencies, and hospitals requiring them to pay for and otherwise provide interpreter services.[31]

The difficulties in effecting change through litigation cannot be ignored. The legislative process is usually less expensive and time-consuming. In either case, links of communication and understanding must be established between all who have roles to play in mental health services for deaf people: legislators, jurists, mental health workers, concerned citizens, and deaf people themselves. They must work together to find good solutions.

Notes

1. Rehabilitation Services Administration, *Third Annual Conference on Deafness, RSA Region III, Ocean City, Md.* (Washington, D.C.: U.S. Department of Health, Education, and Welfare, 1977).

2. J. D. Rainer, K. A. Altshuler, F. J. Kallmann, and W. E. Demming, *Family and Mental Health Problems in a Deaf Population* (New York: Columbia University, New York State Psychiatric Institute, Department of Medical Genetics, 1963), p. 201.

3. M. Vernon, "Techniques of Screening for Mental Illness Among Deaf Clients," *Journal of Rehabilitation of the Deaf* 2(1969): 24.

4. R. R. Grinker, *Psychiatric Diagnosis, Therapy, and Research on the Psychotic Deaf* (Washington, D.C.: U.S. Department of Health, Education, and Welfare, Social and Rehabilitation Service, 1969), p. 24.

5. People ex. rel Meyers v. Briggs, 46 Ill. 2d 281, 263 N.E. 2d 109 (1970)

6. People v. Lang, 26 Ill. App. 3d 648 (1975), 325 N.E. 2d 305 (1975)

7. People v. Lang, 62 Ill. App. 3d 688 (1978), 378 N.E. 2d 1106 (1978)

8. Jackson v. Indiana, 406 U.S. 715 (1972)

9. Dusky v. United States, 362 U.S. 402 (1960)

10. L. Robinson, "Group Psychotherapy Using Manual Communication," *Mental Hospitals* 16(1965): 172–174; and L. Robinson, "A Program for Deaf Mental Patients," *Hospital and Community Psychiatry* 24(1973): 40–42.

11. O'Connor v. Donaldson, 442 U.S. 563 (1975)

12. Covington v. Harris, 419 *Federal Supplement* 617 (D.C. Cir. 1969) at 623

13. In re Henry Jones, 338 F. Supp. 428 (D.D.C. 1972) at 429

14. Covington v. Harris

15. Wyatt v. Stickney, 325 F. Supp. 781 (M.D. Ala. 1970), 344 F. Supp. 373 (1972); aff'd. sub. nom. Wyatt v. Aderholt, 503 F.2d 1305 (5th Cir. 1974)

16. New York State Association for Retarded Children, Inc. v. Carey, 393 F. Supp. 715 (E.D.N.Y. 1975) at 718

17. 373 F.2d 451 (D.C. Cir. 1967)

18. D.C. Code §21-562 (1966)

19. Community Mental Health Centers Construction Act, 42 *United States Code* §2689

20. *Preliminary Report* (Washington, D.C.: President's Commission on Mental Health, 1977), p. 8.

21. 405 F. Supp. 974 (D.D.C. 1975)

22. Wouri v. Zitnay, No. 75-80-SD (S.D. Maine, July 14, 1978)

23. Pennhurst State School and Hospital v. Halderman, 101 S. Ct. 1531 (1981)

24. 42 U.S.C. §6000

25. 42 U.S.C. §6010

26. Georgia S.B. 449, Act 1359 (1978)

27. Illinois Mental Health Code S.B. 250, 252, 253, 255; the amendment passed the Illinois legislature as H.B. 1612, Sept. 21, 1977.

28. Massachusetts General Laws Ann. Ch. 123 §4 (1974)

29. Pennsylvania Statute Ann. Tit. 50 §7107 (1976)

30. 45 *Code of Federal Regulations* §84.52(d)

31. E.g., Camenisch v. University of Texas, 616 F.2d 127 (5th Cir. 1980), vacated as moot 451 U.S. 390 (1981); Crawford v. University of North Carolina, 440 F. Supp. 1047 (M.D.N.C. 1977); Herbold v. The Trustees of California State Universities and Colleges, C-78-1358 RHS (N.D. Cal. 1978); Riker v. Holy Cross Hospital, 78-1437 (D. Md. 1978); and Williams v. Quern, 78-C-656 (N.D. Ill. 1978).

CHAPTER SEVEN
Employment

Until recently the rights of disabled people to employment were largely unprotected. A Senate report accompanying the Rehabilitation Act Amendments of 1974 noted that disabled people are "barred from employment" and "underemployed because of archaic statutes and laws."[1]

This deplorable condition is evident in the economic status of the deaf population.[2] A number of studies indicate that deaf people suffer underemployment and lower incomes because of their disability.[3] "They quickly reach a plateau, and there they remain," Allen Sussman and Larry Stewart state.

> Everywhere we find deaf men and women of normal or above-average abilities operating automatic machines, performing simple assembly line operations, or otherwise occupied in unchallenging routines. This stereotyping illustrates the discriminatory attitudes toward the deaf job applicants that are inevitable among slightly informed professionals.[4]

Automation poses some very special problems for the disabled person in the labor force. Disabled workers, particularly deaf people, tend to be more heavily concentrated in occupations where automation is making its greatest inroads. Nearly 50 percent of all deaf employees are in manufacturing.[5]

Employer attitudes create the largest single barrier to employment opportunities. Employers often have stereotyped assumptions that underestimate the capabilities of a disabled person. One study indicated that disabled people must generally be more qualified or competent than nondisabled people in order to overcome negative attitudes and assumptions.[6] Employers often refuse to hire disabled people because of unjustified fears that a disabled person cannot perform the job safely. Studies of the safety of both mentally and physically disabled people in the employment setting indicate that these fears are groundless.[7]

Employers use communication barriers as the reason for limiting job

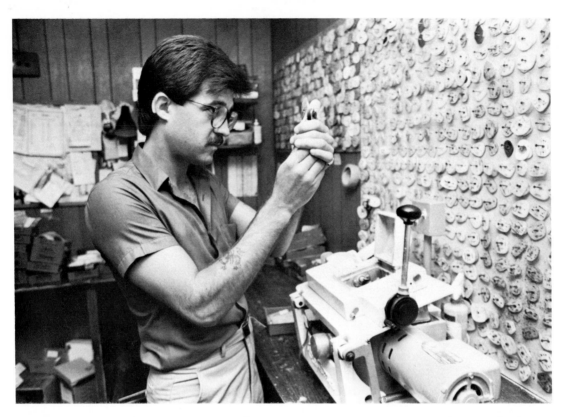

opportunities for deaf applicants and employees. But communication difficulties "are often exaggerated, and fairly effective substitutes for oral communication are disregarded."[8] Inability to use the telephone is often given as a reason not to consider a deaf applicant, even when use of a phone is not an essential part of the job. In jobs requiring only occasional telephone communication, minor changes in assignment of job responsibilities can accommodate the deaf worker. For example, a deaf worker assumes some of a hearing coworker's responsibilities while the hearing person answers the phones.

If a job requires significant telephone contact with one other office, a reasonable accommodation may be to install a telecommunications device in both offices, thus allowing the deaf employee to perform all job duties including those requiring telephone communication. In supervisory positions, a secretary or interpreter can answer the telephone and facilitate the conversation either through lipreading, notes, or sign language, whichever is the preferred method of the deaf person.

The requirement of attendance at various meetings or conferences is also used as a reason not to consider deaf applicants. But reasonable accommodations, such as interpreters, can enable deaf workers to participate fully in group meetings and training sessions.

Title V Remedies

Today, there are a variety of federal statutory remedies available to combat employment discrimination. Those remedies are found primarily in Sections 501, 503, and 504 of Title V of the Rehabilitation Act of 1973. While they are similar in many respects, each of these three sections of the law differs somewhat in application, scope, and quality. Each applies to different types of employers: Section 501 to the federal government, Section 503 to companies that do business with the federal government (federal contractors), and Section 504 to recipients of federal financial assistance. Each imposes varying levels of responsibility upon employers. Sections 501 and 503 require affirmative action, while Section 504 imposes only a duty of nondiscrimination. Section 504 allows an aggrieved individual to go directly to federal court to enforce his or her statutory rights, while Sections 501 and 503 require the individual to first file an administrative complaint. They also differ in the procedures to be followed in filing an administrative complaint. When faced with employment discrimination based on handicap, one must determine which of the three sections applies.

'Qualified' Disabled Person

The Rehabilitation Act does not guarantee jobs for all handicapped people. Instead, it prohibits discrimination in employment against handicapped people who are "qualified" for a job. The definition of a qualified person differs slightly under the three parts of the act:

- The Section 501 regulation for federal employees describes a qualified handicapped person as a handicapped person who, with or without reasonable accommodation, can perform the essential functions of the position in question without endangering the health and safety of the individual or others.[9]

- The Section 503 regulation for federal contractors refers to a qualified handicapped individual as one who is "capable of performing a particular job, with reasonable accommodation to his or her handicap."[10]

- The Section 504 regulation defines a qualified handicapped person as one who "with reasonable accommodation, can perform the essential functions of the job in question."[11]

In all of these definitions, the two central questions in determining whether a handicapped person is qualified for a specific position are (1) What are the essential functions of the job? and (2) Are there reasonable accommodations that will make it possible for a handicapped person to perform the essential functions of the job?

Essential Functions

The regulations for Sections 501, 503, and 504 do not define what is meant by "essential functions." The concept is critical, though, in making certain that employers do not disqualify handicapped people just because these people have difficulty with a task that is only marginally related to the job. For example, a deaf person considered for a typing position should not be disqualified because he or she has trouble using the telephone. The essential function is typing.

In practice, essential functions for a job must be determined on a case-by-case basis. This analysis is complicated by the employer's duty to restructure the job, including rewriting job descriptions, if necessary, to eliminate nonessential tasks that are barriers for handicapped workers. This is part of the employer's duty to make "reasonable accommodation" to the needs of handicapped workers. In judicial or administrative proceedings, the burden of showing what is essential is on the recipient of federal assistance.

As now written the Section 503 regulation does not use the term "essential functions" but instead considers people qualified if they are able to do a "particular job" with reasonable accommodation. This may be a more restrictive definition since it implies that handicapped people must perform all functions of the job, including those that are nonessential tasks. But Sections 501, 503, and 504 all require employers to make reasonable accommodations for handicapped employees, including job restructuring, so the difference in the definition of "qualified" may be illusory. Amendments have been proposed to bring Section 503's language into conformity with that of Section 504.[12]

Reasonable accommodations for deaf people might include telecommunications devices, oscilloscopes to allow them to communicate telephonically with a computer, interpreters, and telephone amplifiers. This list is not all-inclusive but merely a guide. The ap-

---

Reasonable Accomodations

The regulations for Sections 501, 503, and 504 all list the following as possible reasonable accommodations in employment:

- Making facilities used by employees—work benches, parking lots, telephones, lavatories, and entrances, for example—readily accessible to and usable by handicapped people;

- Restructuring jobs in order to reassign nonessential tasks;

- Arranging part-time or modified work schedules;

- Acquiring or modifying equipment or machinery;

- Providing readers for blind employees and interpreters for deaf employees.[13]

propriate accommodation depends on the needs of the particular disabled worker and the particular job he or she is performing. With advances in modern technology and management science, relatively inexpensive devices and techniques for accommodating handicapped workers are increasingly available.

Reasonable accommodations are often a matter of common sense. For example, a deaf welder worked in an outdoor yard where trucks delivered fruit bins. His supervisor fired him be-

cause he believed the man could not work there safely. Later the supervisor realized that the deaf employee could be stationed to see any danger from the trucks entering the yard. With this accommodation, and with fellow employees informed of his deafness, the man could safely perform his job in a fully satisfactory manner.

Another case involved a hearing-impaired woman who had difficulty working in one part of her office because background noise interfered with her hearing aid. When she was

reassigned to a quieter part of the office, her difficulty was reduced and her productivity increased.

Sometimes employers do not wish to hire deaf workers because they claim that deaf workers will not be able to hear fire alarms and warning devices on machinery. These employers can make a simple accommodation by installing a light that flashes when the alarm or buzzer sounds.

In the federal workplace, the Civil Service Reform Act of 1978 and the *Federal Personnel Manual* also provide reasonable accommodations for deaf federal employees by specifically authorizing agency heads to employ or assign interpreters to deaf employees.[14]

Employer Exemptions

Under Sections 501 and 504, a recipient employer does not have to provide a reasonable accommodation if it would cause "undue hardship" on the program's operation. The factors that determine if there is an undue hardship are

- The overall size of the recipient's program with respect to number of employees, number and type of facilities, and size of budget;

- The nature of the recipient's operation, including the composition and structure of the recipient's workforce; and

- The type and cost of the accommodation needed.[15]

The "Analysis to the Section 504

Regulation" gives some examples of factors to be weighed in determining if an accommodation causes undue hardship:

> (A) small day-care center might not be required to expend more than a nominal sum, such as that necessary to equip a telephone for use by a secretary with impaired hearing, but a large school district might be required to make available a teacher's aid to a blind applicant for a teaching job. Further, it might be considered reasonable to require a state welfare agency to accommodate a deaf employee by providing an interpreter, while it would constitute an undue hardship to impose that requirement on a provider of foster home care services.[16]

Section 503 has a similar defense for employers but uses the term "business necessity" instead of "undue hardship." The same factors apply in determining either a business necessity or an undue hardship. Either one, if proven, excuses an employer from providing a reasonable accommodation.

Medical Examinations

Deaf people are sometimes denied particular jobs on the basis of medical criteria that disqualify any person with a hearing loss. Deaf people have been medically disqualified as bus mechanics or geologists solely on the basis of their hearing loss. These blanket medical exclusions can be challenged if they are not job related. In addition, under Section 504 regulations an employer may make offers of employment to handicapped people dependent upon the results of medical examinations only if such examinations are administered in a nondiscriminatory manner to all employees and the results are treated on a confidential basis.[17]

Job Training Programs

Sometimes deaf people are refused interpreters for training programs that are a prerequisite for employment or are essential for retaining or advancing in their jobs. This violates Sections 501, 503, and 504. The Office of Personnel Management will provide interpreters for all deaf federal employees participating in its training programs. The comptroller general for the United States also has decided that special expenses will be provided for sign language interpreters when necessary for deaf employees to participate in government training courses.

Employers with federal contracts frequently contract out to independent groups to conduct training. If the independent group does not provide interpreters, the contract can be challenged. A recipient of federal assistance cannot participate contractually or in other relationships with groups that discriminate against qualified disabled people.[18]

Some employers hire deaf people only for certain jobs such as working with loud machines. The U.S. Postal Service has encouraged this hiring practice. Section 503, however, prohibits designating certain jobs for deaf employees. Deaf workers cannot be "ghettoized" in one job category.[19]

Furthermore, Sections 501 and 503 require employers to make special recruitment efforts to comply with their affirmative action responsibilities. For deaf people, this includes advertising in newspapers directed toward deaf audiences, recruiting at schools for the deaf, and advertising with deaf clubs and organizations.[20]

Section 503 also requires companies to internally disseminate their policy of affirmatively recruiting and promoting qualified handicapped workers. The notification must be written at a language level the average deaf person can understand.[21]

Affirmative Action

The major substantive difference between the three employment sections of the Rehabilitation Act is that Sections 501 and 503 require the federal government and federal contractors to take affirmative action to hire, promote, or retain qualified handicapped persons. Section 504, however, does not require affirmative action; it simply requires nondiscrimination.

The difference between affirmative action and nondiscrimination is a fine one. Affirmative action characteristically means special programs to actively recruit, hire, train, accommodate, and promote qualified disabled people. Under Sections 501 and 503, the federal government and federal contractors must establish and implement such programs. Nondiscrimination, on the other hand, usually means a more

passive obligation to treat disabled employees in the same manner as other employees.

In many situations, however, identical treatment may itself be discriminatory. An employer who holds a staff meeting for all employees has effectively excluded a deaf employee from participating if no interpreter is provided. The same is true of an employer who hires a person in a wheelchair but does not have ramps in the building to allow the employee to get to work. By treating the disabled employee the same as the nondisabled employee, the employer has acted unfairly. In all situations in which identical treatment

constitutes discrimination against disabled employees, Section 504 requires recipients of federal financial assistance to take specific steps to provide equal opportunity and *equally effective* means of taking advantage of that opportunity.

Federal Obligations

The federal government has established several policies and programs designed to fulfill its affirmative action obligations under Section 501. For example, the government will make special arrangements for applicants taking the Civil Service examination when the applicant's disability prevents him or her from competing equally. These include provision of readers for blind applicants and interpreters for deaf applicants, waiver of certain verbal tests for deaf applicants, provision of enlarged answer blocks for applicants with poor manual dexterity or motor coordination, provision of taped and/or brailled tests, and extension of time limits for taking the tests.

The government also has special hiring programs designed to facilitate the appointment of disabled employees. One hiring program is the temporary trial appointment, which gives the disabled employee an opportunity to know what he or she can do and overcome the employer's anxieties about the person's capabilities. Under this program, physically and mentally disabled people can be hired for a four-month period without going through the normal competitive hiring procedures. As soon as the employee has demonstrated his or her ability to do the job, the appointment can be made permanent, although no guarantees are given.

Another program used to hire disabled individuals is known as the "excepted" or "Schedule A" appointment. It is available to both severely physically disabled and mentally retarded applicants. Under the excepted appointment program, disabled people can be hired for permanent jobs by federal agencies without having to take the Civil Service examination. The purpose of the program is to avoid the discriminatory effects of the examination.

There is one basic problem with the excepted appointment program: An excepted appointee lacks the same employment benefits and job security as an employee hired under the regular merit-system procedures. Although an excepted appointee's job is "permanent," he or she can be fired, demoted, or suspended without a hearing or other due process protections. Excepted appointees are also denied equal transfer rights, equal opportunity to compete for promotions, and equal protection in the event of a general job lay off (e.g., reduction-in-force).

Legal Challenges

Several lawsuits have challenged this

basic inequity in the excepted appointment program. For example, on January 8, 1982, the District of Columbia federal Court of Appeals held that the federal government violated Section 501 by denying equal employment rights to an excepted service employee at the National Aeronautics and Space Administration (NASA).[22] The case was filed by the National Association of the Deaf Legal Defense Fund (NADLDF) on behalf of Edward Shirey, a deaf excepted service employee who was terminated in a reduction-in-force by NASA in January 1978. Solely because of his handicapped, excepted-service status, Shirey was not given the same rights as competitive service employees to find another job with NASA or the federal government. The appeals court ruled that it is discriminatory to deny equal rights to handicapped individuals when they are equally qualified and performing the same work as competitive service employees.

The rules applying to handicapped excepted service employees have changed in the last few years, but one change came too late to help Shirey. In March 1979 President Carter signed Executive Order 12125, which authorized handicapped excepted service employees to convert to the competitive service after two years of satisfactory performance in their jobs. But this new rule did not apply to Mr. Shirey, who was terminated in January 1978. Despite the fact that he had worked for more than four years in the same job as

his competitive service co-workers and had received satisfactory ratings, he was still denied equal rights. Such a policy violates Section 501, said the appeals court. Its decision reversed a federal district court ruling which found no violation of Section 501.

Following its obligation under Section 501 and the Civil Service Reform Act of 1978, the federal government has authorized several methods of hiring interpreters for deaf employees in various work situations. Each federal agency has the option of either (1) hiring full-time interpreters, (2) using other employees who can interpret fluently, or (3) contracting out with individual interpreters or interpreter referral agencies on an as-needed basis. The best method depends on the work situation involved. If a particular deaf employee's job requires frequent use of an interpreter, or if there are several deaf employees in one agency whose combined needs require frequent service, then a full-time interpreter on staff would be the best solution. If an interpreter is needed for an occasional or regular office meeting, it might be best to contract for services of a private interpreter.

Further Assistance

More detailed information on the procedures for taking advantage of all these special federal programs and services can be obtained by contacting federal job information centers throughout the country. Also, the personnel office of each federal agency has a selective placement coordinator who is responsible for implementing these programs.

These federal selective placement coordinators want advice and need assistance from vocational rehabilitation counselors on all issues and problems involving recruitment, hiring, and accommodations for disabled employees. Rehabilitation counselors should develop contacts with federal personnel offices; they should be thoroughly familiar with federal hiring practices and job application procedures. Continuing interaction among counselors, selective placement coordinators, managers, and supervisors is essential.

Enforcement Procedures
Section 501: Federal Government

A disabled federal employee or applicant for federal employment who believes he or she has been discriminated against by a federal agency can file an administrative complaint with that agency. There are strict time limits imposed for each step of the procedure. While waiver of the time limits is sometimes allowed for good cause, a complaint can be rejected for failure to meet the deadline. The disabled person has the right to be represented by an attorney at all stages of the complaint process. If a deaf complainant needs an interpreter at any stage of the proceed-

---

The federal government has suggested ways that rehabilitation counselors can take the initiative to ensure that affirmative action is implemented:[23]

- Survey federal agencies to determine what types of jobs are likely to be available and which of these are likely to be in demand by disabled individuals.

- Work with other counselors and organizations to establish referral systems.

- Provide follow-up assistance to agency supervisors after a disabled person has been hired.

- Arrange for selective placement coordinators, managers, and supervisors to tour rehabilitation and independent living centers and to attend workshops and consciousness-raising programs.

- Give recognition awards and publicity to agencies that actively participate in employment programs for disabled individuals.

- Share information about federal job vacancies and personnel needs with rehabilitation counselors in the area.

- And involve selective placement coordinators in the activities of rehabilitation agencies.

---

ings, the agency must provide and pay for one.

The step-by-step administrative complaint process is as follows:[24]

A. Informal Pre-complaint Counseling

1. An employee or applicant for employment must contact the agency's equal employment opportunity (EEO) office within thirty days of the discriminatory act. The contact may be made in person or by letter. No form is required.

2. The EEO office will assign an EEO counselor to the case. The person bringing the complaint (complainant) must provide all the information about the discriminatory policy or action to the EEO counselor.

3. The role of the EEO counselor is to:
   a. make an inquiry into the complaint and discuss it with all the people involved;
   b. attempt an informal resolution within twenty-one days;
   c. not discourage the complainant from filing a formal complaint; and
   d. not reveal the identity of the complainant unless authorized to do so.

4. If informal resolution cannot be achieved, the EEO counselor will send the complainant a "Notice of Final Interview" informing him or her of the right to file a formal complaint.

5. The complainant has the right to file a formal complaint anytime *after twenty-one days* from the date the EEO counselor was first contacted. The complainant need *not* wait for a "Notice of Final Interview" letter before filing the formal complaint.

6. The EEO counselor, in most cases, has no authority to force managment to settle the complaint. The counselor can only try to help negotiate a settlement. Unless it appears that this pre-complaint counseling may produce a settlement, the complainant should file his or her formal complaint immediately upon expiration of the twenty-one-day settlement period.

B. Formal Complaint

1. A complainant can file a formal complaint anytime after the twenty-one-day settlement period has elapsed, but not later than *fifteen* days after receipt of the "Notice of Final Interview" letter from the EEO counselor.

2. Content of formal complaint
   a. The formal complaint is written on a form provided by the agency's EEO office and is filed with that office.
   b. The written complaint

should discuss in detail all of the facts involved and should include copies of letters and other documents substantiating those facts.

c. If there is a continuing pattern or policy of discrimination, the complainant should describe the discriminatory activity as "continuing" in order to avoid any time-deadline problems.

3. Rejection of complaint
   a. The agency may reject the entire complaint or some of the issues raised if:
      i. it is not filed on time,
      ii. the complaint raises matters identical to another complaint of the employee,
      iii. the complainant is not an employee or applicant of the agency, or
      iv. the complaint is not based on disability discrimination.
   b. If the agency rejects the complaint, the complainant must be notified in writing. The employee may then appeal to the Equal Employment Opportunity Commission (EEOC) *within fifteen days* or file suit in federal district court *within thirty days* of receipt of the rejection letter.

4. Investigation of complaint

a. If the agency accepts the complaint, it must properly investigate. The agency will appoint an EEO investigator, a person other than the EEO counselor.
b. The investigator will conduct an in-depth inquiry, take sworn affidavits from the people involved, and gather documents and statistics.
c. If the complainant believes that important witnesses have not been interviewed or that important evidence has not been explored, then he or she should notify the investigator in writing.

5. Adjustment of complaint
   When the investigation is completed, the investigator writes a report. The EEO office sends copies of the report to both the complainant and the employer and provides them an opportunity to informally adjust (settle) the matter on the basis of the results of the investigation. If the complaint is informally adjusted, the terms of the adjustment must be in writing.

6. Proposed disposition
   a. If the complaint cannot be adjusted, then the agency will issue a proposed disposition (decision).
   b. If the complainant is satisfied with the proposed dis-

position, the agency must then implement the terms of the disposition.

c. If the complainant is dissatisfied with the proposed disposition, he or she may request a hearing before the EEOC in writing *within fifteen days* or file suit in federal district court *within* *thirty days* of receipt of the proposed disposition.

7. EEOC hearing

a. At the hearing, as at all other stages in the process, the complainant has the right to be represented by an attorney and to have a qualified interpreter.

b. On the basis of evidence submitted at the hearing, the examiner (judge) will issue a recommended decision that the agency can reverse.

c. If the complainant is dissatisfied with the decision, he or she may appeal within fifteen days to the EEOC Office of Review and Appeals or file suit in federal court within thirty days of receipt of the decision.

d. If the decision is that the agency has discriminated, i.e., if the complainant wins, he or she may be awarded back pay and attorney's fees.

C. Right to Sue in Federal Court

1. The complainant can file suit in federal district court at any time after *180 days* from the date the *formal* EEO complaint was filed, if the agency has not yet issued a *final* decision.

2. In addition, as noted above, the complainant can file suit within thirty days after completion of other stages of the administrative process (e.g., after receipt of the notice of proposed disposition or after receipt of final agency action).

Section 503: Federal Contractors

Section 503 of the Rehabilitation Act

requires employers who have contracts with the federal government for more than $2,500 to take affirmative action to hire and promote qualified disabled people. About 300,000 private businesses are subject to Section 503. The work performed under these contracts includes construction of government buildings, repair of federal highways, and leasing of government buildings, to name a few. In addition to primary contractors, Section 503 covers companies which have subcontracted for more than $2,500 of federal business from a primary contractor.

The administrative complaint procedure under Section 503 differs significantly from that described under Section 501. Section 503 is enforced by the U.S. Department of Labor's Office of Federal Contract Compliance Programs (OFCCP). An applicant or employee who believes he or she has been discriminated against by a federal contractor can file a written complaint with the regional OFCCP office within 180 days of the date of the alleged violation. The regional OFCCP is supposed to investigate promptly and attempt to resolve the complaint. If the regional OFCCP finds no violation of Section 503, then the complainant may appeal to the national OFCCP office in Washington, D.C., within thirty days. If the regional OFCCP finds that the employer has in fact violated Section 503, then an attempt is made to resolve the matter informally and provide the appropriate relief to the complainant.

If the employer refuses to provide the appropriate relief, OFCCP can then employ more formal enforcement mechanisms. These include bringing suit in federal court, withholding payments due on existing federal contracts, termination of existing federal contracts, and/or barring the contractor from receiving future federal contracts. If OFCCP begins any of these enforcement methods, the employer can request a formal administrative hearing. While the complainant can participate in the administrative hearing, it is primarily a dispute between OFCCP and the employer. Like the Section 501 EEO complaint procedure, the OFCCP process is long and time consuming.

An individual's right to go directly to court and enforce a Section 503 claim is not spelled out in the Section 503 regulations and has not yet been firmly established by the courts. However, strong legal arguments can be made by analogy to Section 504, where the right to sue has been established. Courts that have addressed this issue in recent years have been divided.[25]

Section 504: Federal Financial Recipients

The procedures for enforcing Section 504 are discussed in Chapter Two, pages 20–24. As noted there, Section 504 applies to all recipients of federal financial assistance. "Federal financial assistance" under Section 504 differs from a "federal contract" under Section

503. It can mean grants and loans of federal money, services of federal personnel, or the lease of federal buildings for less than fair market value. Because of widespread dependence on federal money, recipients of federal financial assistance are many and varied.

Before receiving such assistance, all recipients must sign an "assurance of compliance" form agreeing to obey Section 504.

The U.S. government as well as advocacy groups for disabled people have always taken the position that Section 504 prohibits employment discrimination by all recipients of federal aid, regardless of the purpose for which their federal funds are to be used. In other words, if a hospital received federal funds to buy medical equipment, Section 504 covers that hospital's employment practices.

Some courts, however, have tried to limit Section 504's employment discrimination coverage only to those recipients for whom the primary purpose of their federal financial assistance is to promote employment. Under this circumscribed interpretation, the hospital that receives federal funds to buy equipment is free to discriminate against disabled job applicants and employees. Section 504 would apply to the hospital's employment practices only if the hospital received federal funds (such as a Comprehensive Employment Training Act grant) whose primary purpose is to provide jobs for unemployed and low-income people.[26]

State Statutes

State laws sometimes provide a remedy for employment discrimination when the Rehabilitation Act does not apply. A number of states have recently acted to add some category such as "physical or mental handicap" to the list of classes protected by traditional human rights and employment discrimination laws. Formerly these laws covered only race, sex, and religion. These laws are useful because they often apply to all public and private employers, thereby prohibiting discrimination even by employers who do not have federal contracts or grants.

There is no uniformity in state human rights laws. Some protect physically disabled workers but not mentally disabled ones. Some require reasonable accommodations to disabled workers, but most do not. Some allow private causes of action—the right of individuals to sue in state court; others are limited to administrative enforcement by underfunded public agencies. In most states the agency charged with enforcement is the state civil rights commission or state employment agency. Enforcement procedures and remedies vary widely, as do the definitions of protected disabilities and of covered employers.[27]

Vocational Rehabilitation Services

Because of the chronic underemployment problems of deaf people, vocational services are widely needed and heavily used. The Rehabilitation Act is the principle federal law providing rehabilitation services for disabled people. The Rehabilitation Services Administration (RSA), part of the U.S. Department of Education, is the primary agency for implementing the section of the act which deals with disabled people.

Title I of the act provides federal grants to states for meeting the vocational needs of their disabled citizens.[28] To be eligible, a state vocational rehabilitation agency submits a state service plan for approval by RSA. The plan must comply with Title I provisions and RSA regulations.[29] To receive the grants, the state vocational rehabilitation (VR) agencies must agree to prescribe and write an individual rehabilitation plan for each person eligible under the act for the service. For deaf people, VR services include vocational counseling, education and training, medical services, job placement, job support, and provision of interpreters and telecommunication devices.

Amendments to the Rehabilitation Act in 1978 broadened the services available to deaf people.[30] The RSA Office of Handicapped Individuals was given authority to fund twelve programs for interpreter training.[31] The secretary of education was authorized to set minimum standards for interpreter certification, and the programs were also permitted to train teachers of deaf students. Congress appropriated $900,000 for the first year of this program. Ten programs have been funded.

The amendments also provided for use of discretionary funds from the RSA commissioner to set up information and interpreter referral centers in each state. The centers may be run by public agencies or nonprofit organizations that provide services to deaf people. The centers must serve the whole state and be centrally located.

Any public agency serving deaf people can use the interpreter referral services. The funds of these referral centers may also be used for the purchase or rental of telecommunications devices. When the program needs outside help for its operation, it is required to seek it from private, nonprofit organizations either comprised primarily of hearing-impaired people or having the primary purpose of providing services to hearing-impaired people.

Comprehensive rehabilitation centers were also authorized. Their purpose is to provide a broad range of services to disabled people: information and referral, counseling, job placement, health, education, and social and recreational services.[32] Information and technical assistance, including interpreter services, are to be provided by these centers to other public and nonprofit organizations or agencies in the area to help them fulfill their responsibilities under Section 504 of the Rehabilitation Act.

These amendments expand the rehabilitation services available to deaf people and increase the number of public agencies existing to serve their needs.

Notes

1. S. Rep. No. 1297, 93rd Congress, 2nd Session 43 (1974); reprinted in *Congressional and Administrative News*, p. 6400 (1974)

2. See S. Fisher, *An Assessment of the Occupational Status and Training of Former Model Post-Secondary Deaf Students*, unpublished thesis (Washington, D.C.: Gallaudet College, 1974); A. Crammatte, *The Formidable Peak: A Study of Deaf People in Professional Employment* (Washington, D.C.: Gallaudet College, 1965); and E. Boatner, E. Stuckless, and D. Moores, *Occupational Status of the Young Deaf Adult of New England and the Need and Demand for a Regional Technical Vocational Training Center* (West Hartford, Conn.: American School for the Deaf, 1964).

3. A 1978 study showed a significant economic decline for deaf people between 1972 and 1977. Jerome Schein, Director of the Deafness Research and Training Center at New York University, noted that the percentage of deaf people who were working dropped from 65.5 percent in 1972 to 61.3 percent in 1977. These declines ran counter to national trends; for the same period, the national percentages of both men and women who were in the labor force increased. Unemployment for deaf people increased from 9.6 percent in 1972 to 10.9 percent in 1977. Personal income of deaf people as a proportion of the national per capita average declined substantially from 1971 to 1976. In 1971 the average deaf person's personal income was 74.6 percent of the national per capita average; by 1976 this average had dropped to 64.2 percent. This data is from J. Schein, *Economic Status of Deaf Adults* (unpublished study, 1978).

4. A. Sussman and L. Stewart, "Social and Psychological Problems of Deaf People," in *Counseling of Deaf People*, Sussman and Stewart, eds. (New York: New York University School of Education, 1971), p. 25.

5. Schein and Delk, *Deaf Population*, p. 81.

6. Richard, Triandis, and Patterson, "Indices of Employer Prejudice Toward Disabled Applicants," *Journal of Applied Psychology* 45 (1953): 52.

7. See Wolfe, "Disability is No Handicap for Dupont," *The Alliance Review* (Winter, 1973–74): 13; and Kalenick, "Myths About Hiring the Physically Handicapped," *Job Safety and Health* 2(1974): 9, 11.

8. Crammatte, *The Formidable Peak*, p. 118.

9. 29 *Code of Federal Regulations* §1613.702(f)

10. 29 C.F.R. §32.3

11. 45 C.F.R. §84.3(k)(1)

12. 45 *Federal Register* 86,208, December 30, 1980

13. 45 C.F.R. §84.12(b)(2); 29 C.F.R. §1613.704(b)

14. 5 U.S.C. §5331

15. 45 C.F.R. §84.12(c)

16. 42 Fed. Reg. 22,688, May 4, 1977

17. 45 C.F.R. §84.14(c, d)

18. 45 C.F.R. §84.11(a)(4)

19. 41 C.F.R. §60-741.5(i)(2); see also A. Hermann and L. Walker, *Handbook of Employment Rights for the Handicapped: Sections 503 and 504 of the Rehabilitation Act of 1973* (Washington, D.C.: George Washington University, 1978).

20. 41 C.F.R. §60-741.5(f)

21. 41 C.F.R. §60-741

22. Shirey v. Devine, 670 F.2d 1188 (D.C. Cir. 1982)

23. See Office of Personnel Management, "Handbook of Selective Placement of Persons with Physical and Mental Handicaps," OPM Doc. 125-11-3 (March 1979).

24. For more detailed information, see 29 C.F.R. §1613.201 through 1613.806.

25. For court rulings that there is no private right to sue under Section 503, see Rogers v. Frito-Lay, 611 F.2d 1074 (5th Cir. 1980); Simpson v. Reynolds Metal Co., 629 F.2d 1226 (7th Cir. 1980); Simon v. St. Louis County, 656 F.2d 316 (8th Cir. 1981); and Davis v. United Air Lines, No. 81-7093 (2nd Cir. 1981). For court rulings that an individual may bring suit under Section 503, see Hart v. County of Alameda, 485 F. Supp. 66 (N.D. Cal. 1979); and Chaplin v. Consolidated Edison of New York, 482 F. Supp. 1165 (S.D. N.Y. 1980).

26. It is important to note that this limitation applies only to employment discrimination under Section 504, not to discrimination in the provision of services or to program accessibility. For court rulings that there is no private right to sue under Section 504 for employment discrimination because the primary objective of the federal financial assistance involved was not to provide employment, see Trageser v. Libbie Rehabilitation Center, 590 F.2d 87 (4th Cir. 1978), cert denied 442 U.S. 947 (1979); and Carmi v. Metropolitan St. Louis Sewer District, 620 F.2d 672 (8th Cir. 1980), cert denied 449 U.S. 892 (1980). The contrary result was reached in LeStrange v. Consolidated Rail Corp., 687 F.2d 767 (3rd Cir. 1982), cert granted No. 82-862 (1983); Jones v. Metropolitan Atlanta Rapid Transit Authority, 681 F.2d 1376 (5th Cir. 1982), petition for cert filed 51 U.S.L.W. 3535 (U.S. Jan. 11, 1983) (No. 82-1159); and in Hart v. County of Alameda, cited in note 25 above. As the second edition of this book goes to press, the U.S. Supreme Court is preparing to decide this significant issue in Consolidated Rail Corp. v. Darrone, No. 82-862.

27. *Amicus* 3 (1978): 39.

28. 29 U.S.C. §720 *et seq.*

29. 45 C.F.R. §1361.1 *et seq.*

30. Rehabilitation, Comprehensive Services, and Developmental Disabilities Amendments, Public Law 95-602 (1978), 29 U.S.C. §701 *et seq.*

31. 29 U.S.C. §777(e)

32. 29 U.S.C. §775(a)(1)

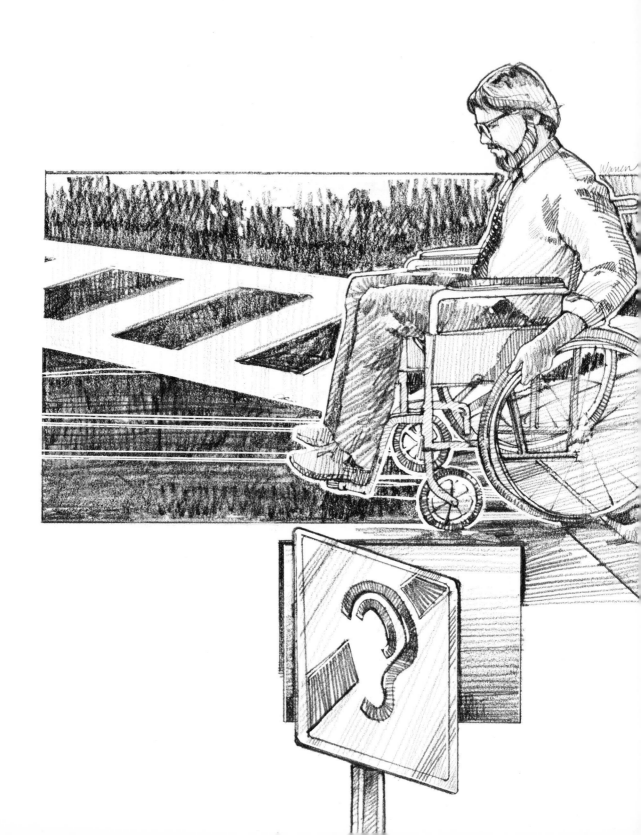

CHAPTER EIGHT
Architectural Barriers

Congress passed Section 502 of the Rehabilitation Act of 1973 to make sure that federally funded buildings are accessible to disabled people.[1] Specifically, Section 502 created an independent federal agency, the Architectural and Transportation Barriers Compliance Board (ATBCB), to enforce the Architectural Barriers Act of 1968. The 1968 law requires most buildings and facilities designed, constructed, altered, or leased with federal money after 1968 to be accessible to disabled people.

This means that buildings cannot have barriers to people who are in wheelchairs or on crutches or who are blind or deaf. Everyone must be able to enter and use these buildings. The potential impact of this law is great. As of 1980, there were 400,000 federally owned and 50,000 federally leased facilities in the United States.

Buildings covered by the Architectural Barriers Act must meet the minimum standards for accessibility established by the American National Standards Institute (ANSI).[2] These standards have also been adopted by the federal government's General Services Administration (GSA).

If a person knows of a federal building that violates these accessibility standards, he or she may file a written complaint with ATBCB, which has the authority to conduct investigations and to attempt to achieve voluntary compliance. If this is not possible, the board's general counsel can file a citation against the federal agency accused of violating the standards. A hearing is held before an administrative law judge to determine if there has been a violation of the barriers act. The judge can order the violating agency to obey the act or withhold or suspend its funding. The judge's order is final and binding on any federal department or agency.

Today's ATBCB

Amendments to Section 502 changed the size and composition of the ATBCB board from only nine federal agency members to ten federal agency members and eleven public members, five of whom must be disabled.[3] The board was also given authority to investigate communication barriers, including the absence of telecommunication devices; to provide technical assistance to make buildings and transportation vehicles accessible; and to adopt its own accessibility standards to replace the ANSI standards.

While ATBCB has achieved voluntary compliance in most of its cases, a number of alleged violations have gone through the citation process. In June 1978 the board ordered the Department of the Interior and the Department of Transportation to re-install two elevators in Washington, D.C.'s Union Station/National Visitors Center to make it accessible to disabled people.

Cases involving pedestrian overpasses and underpasses were successfully settled in St. Louis, Missouri, and Omaha, Nebraska. The St. Louis case marked the first time that federal funds were withheld from the construction of a facility until the question of accessibility was resolved. The Omaha settlement was the first time an agency entered into an agreement to go beyond the requirements of the Architectural Barriers Act and correct existing problems on an agency-wide basis.

In another case, the Department of Health, Education, and Welfare and the General Services Administration were ordered by an administrative law judge to make Alabama's largest office building accessible to disabled persons. The restrooms and elevators in the Birmingham building violated GSA's own ANSI accessibility standards. In his order, the judge stated that cost was no defense for noncompliance. These cases represent the beginning of ATBCB's capacity to ensure accessibility.

Ambiguous Standards

The inadequacy of the twenty-year-old ANSI standards is a serious problem. Although present ANSI standards require accessible and usable public telephones for hearing-impaired individuals, it is not clear whether this entails such specific solutions as amplifiers, telecommunications devices, adapted pay telephones, or adapted telephones in business offices. The requirement of visual warning signals is also unclear. Where should they be? Are flashing exit signs sufficient?

The ATBCB board and GSA are now considering a revised set of accessibility standards that should address the problems of deaf people more specifically. Until new standards are adopted, however, these agencies will continue to use the ANSI standards.

The ambiguity of the ANSI standards lessens the effectiveness of Section 502 for deaf people. However, complaints to the ATBCB board can be used to compel the installation of telecommunication devices. Administrative complaints led to an order that TDDs be installed in post office buildings in several locations. Section 502 can also be used to require the installation of doorbells with flashing-light relays, visual warning systems such as fire alarms, and security systems that are not wholly dependent on operation of an auditory intercom.

The law may also apply to other architectural barriers to communication. For example, this law might be used to compel builders of auditoriums and meetings rooms to install appropri-ate spotlighting for interpreters and audio "loops" to assist persons with hearing aids.

Complaints about architectural, transportation, and communication barriers can be sent to:

Architectural and Transportation
    Barriers Compliance Board
Switzer Building, Room 1010
330 C Street SW
Washington, DC 20201
(202) 245-1801 (Voice or TTY)

In your letter of complaint, identify yourself, the barrier to which you object, the federal agency that is responsible for the building, and the owner and occupant of the building.

Section 504 Compliance

In addition to Section 502, Section 504 can be invoked to remove architectural barriers in structures used by recipients of federal financial assistance. Section 504 regulations at the Departments of Health and Human Services and of Education require each new facility or new part of a facility to be designed and constructed to be readily accessible to and usable by disabled people.[4] Alterations and new construction will comply with Section 504 if they meet the ANSI standards discussed above.

Other federal agencies have adopted the ANSI standards by referring to them in their own Section 504 regulations. If a building is constructed, altered, or leased by the federal government, complaints about architectural barriers could be filed with either the particular federal agency involved under Section 504 or with the ATBCB board under Section 502. If the federal financial assistance was given to a program for some purpose other than construction, alteration, or lease, then, under Section 504, complaints about architectural barriers can only be filed with the particular agency providing the assistance.

Because the ANSI standards do not specifically address many of the communication barriers confronted by deaf people, a person with a complaint about an architectural or communication barrier may have to rely on the general nondiscrimination and program accessibility provisions of Section 504 discussed in Chapter Two.

State Laws

State architectural barrier laws can be used to remove obstructions. Some of these laws are broader in application than the Rehabilitation Act because they are not limited to buildings that receive federal funding. For example, a state or local law may require all newly constructed places of public accommodation to be accessible. If so, this would include restaurants and stores as well as state structures.

Other state laws specifically deal with the problems of deaf people. Some states require apartment buildings to install both auditory and visual smoke detectors and alarms. If a state does not have such a law, deaf people might want to lobby for one.

Notes

1. 29 *United States Code* §792

2. 45 *Code of Federal Regulations* §84.23(c)

3. See Public Law 95-602: The Rehabilitation, Comprehensive Services, and Developmental Disabilities Amendments of 1978; 29 U.S.C. §701 *et seq.*

4. 45 C.F.R. §84.23(a)

CHAPTER NINE
The Legal System

Deaf people experience numerous difficulties with the legal system because of communication barriers. They may be unjustly committed to mental institutions because they are misdiagnosed by people who do not know how to work and communicate with them. They often cannot afford a lawyer; if they can, they often are unable to find one who is able to communicate with them and understand their needs. If they have to go to court, they often do not understand the proceedings and cannot adequately explain their side of the story. More than fifty years ago, a judge wrote:

> [I]n the absence of an interpreter, it would be a physical impossibility for the accused, a deaf [defendant], to know or understand the nature and cause of the accusation against him and . . . he could only stand by helplessly . . . without knowing or understand[ing], and all this in the teeth of the mandatory constitutional rights which apply. Mere confrontation would be useless.[1]

Today's courts still deny equal access and due process to hearing-impaired people. Several of the state interpreter laws are inadequate. They fail to ensure that deaf defendants understand fully the charges against them and participate effectively in their own defense. A number of state interpreter laws fail to provide interpreters for arrest and civil and administrative proceedings. In recent years, however, considerable progress has been made at both federal and state levels to make courts more accessible to deaf people.

Signs of Progress

In 1979 Congress enacted the Bilingual, Hearing, and Speech-Impaired Court Interpreter Act.[2] This law requires that, in any criminal or civil action *initiated by the federal government*, the court must appoint a qualified interpreter. The director of the Administrative Office of the U.S. Courts determines the qualifications required of court-appointed interpreters.

Each district court must maintain on file in the office of the clerk of the court a list of certified interpreters, both oral and manual, for deaf people. The history of the legislation shows that the director of court administration must consult organizations of and for deaf people in preparing such lists. These organizations include the National Association of the Deaf (NAD) and the Registry of Interpreters for the Deaf (RID).

If any interpreter is unable to communicate effectively with the defendant, party, or witness, the court's presiding officer must dismiss that interpreter and obtain the services of another. The service is paid for by the government, whether or not the person needing the service is indigent. In his or her discretion, however, a judge can apportion the interpreter fees among the parties or tax their costs to the losing party.

The shortcoming of this law is that an interpreter is not provided for a deaf person who initiates an action, for example, to challenge a denial of federal rights. Only criminal and civil cases initiated by the federal government require appointment of interpreters.

Many states will provide an interpreter to a deaf defendant in a criminal proceeding, but very few provide one at the time of arrest, even though it is during pretrial proceedings that a deaf person is most often denied his or her constitutional rights. Few states provide interpreters in civil cases.

However, the Department of Justice's analysis of its Section 504 regulation specifically requires the appointment of interpreters in both civil and criminal proceedings:

> Court systems receiving Federal financial assistance shall provide for the availability of qualified interpreters for civil and criminal court proceedings involving persons with hearing or speaking impairments. . . . Where a recipient has an obligation to provide qualified interpreters under this subpart, the recipient has the corresponding responsibility to pay for the services of the interpreters.[3]

Interpreters for indigent deaf defendants are also specifically provided:

> [In cases where the courts appoint counsel for indigents, they] are also required to assign qualfied interpreters (certified, where possible, by recognized certification agencies) in cases involving indigent defendants with hearing or speaking impairments to aid the communication between client and attorney. The availability of interpreting services to the indigent defendant would be required for all phases of the preparation and presentation of the defendant's case.[4]

Miranda *Advice of Rights*

In the landmark decision *Miranda v. Arizona*, the Supreme Court recognized that questioning by police in the stationhouse or jail is inherently coercive and undermines the privilege against self-incrimination.[5] As a result of this decision, police are now required to "effectively inform" the accused person of his or her constitutional rights before any questioning can take place. Without use of a qualified interpreter, most deaf people would not be able to understand their rights fully, and any waiver of their rights would not meet the Supreme Court's standard of being voluntary, knowing, and intelligent.

Depending upon which reading-level formula is used, the standard written advice of rights form given to suspects before questioning requires a sixth-to-eighth-grade reading comprehension level. The ability of the hearing person to understand the rights set forth in this form is not seriously impaired by a reading deficiency, because they can be told out loud what is written on the form. The listening comprehension level of people with normal hearing and of people with reading problems usually exceeds their reading comprehension level.[6] However, the reading level required by the *Miranda* warnings and advice of rights forms remains far above the comprehension of most prelingually deaf people. These people require a careful explanation of the rights by a qualfied sign language interpreter.

The conceptual and linguistic difficulties posed by the *Miranda* advice of rights cannot be overcome by a direct translation into sign language. Sign language uses everyday rather than formal concepts. Critical concepts that are unfamiliar to many deaf people include "right" and "Constitution." Some deaf people would not understand the term "lawyer" in the full sense of understanding a lawyer's function. There are not many signs to express legal terms. The sign for "Constitution" is newly created; most American Sign Language users would be unfamiliar with either the sign or the English word let alone the concept behind it.

> Mary Furey, an educator, observed that the standard advice of rights form poses serious problems for the average deaf person.
>
> A great number of deaf adults would find the language of this [Miranda] warning strange and incomprehensible because of the many idioms used in it. True, each word in and of itself is simple, but when two or more are put together in a special sense, they can be totally unintelligible to a deaf individual because many deaf adults give each word narrow or literal meaning. . . . The idiom "can be used against" would also be difficult to understand. Even the word "rights" could be perplexing.
>
> Infinitives, verbs used in the passive voice, gerunds, and other verbals such as . . . "without a lawyer present," etc., would not be readily comprehended by the usual deaf adult. The meaning of "if" at the beginning of a clause usually is not understood. . . .
>
> I find that . . . the warning itself . . . as presently written, would be difficult for the usual deaf adult to read with understanding and indeed could be misunderstood or not comprehended at all.[7]

Fingerspelling of important legal terms would not necessarily increase understanding, especially if the accused deaf person has a low reading level.[8] To be understood, the terms and their meanings must be carefully explained in clear concepts. A qualified interpreter is fundamental at this point. Acting out and other demonstrative approaches might be needed.

Moreover, deaf people are accustomed to questions that are direct and concrete. Several of the rights described in the *Miranda* warning are mentioned as if implied to exist. The word "if" is frequently used.

Examples of the Problem

In a recent case, a Maryland circuit court addressed the problem of communicating the *Miranda* advice of rights to a deaf defendant. David Barker, a congenitally deaf man with a reading comprehension level of grade 2.8, was charged with murder in 1975. The charges were dropped, but in 1976, while Barker was in custody for unrelated charges, police questioned him extensively about the murder by means of written notes. They did so without providing him either a sign language interpreter or advice of counsel. After several hours of being questioned, Barker signed the *Miranda* waiver of rights and then a confession.

When Barker was interrogated a month later with an interpreter, he showed confusion in answering questions. Asked if he had understood the

Miranda advice of rights, he replied in sign language, "a little bit." He also referred to promises allegedly made by the police guaranteeing hospitalization.

The court suppressed the first confession as being involuntary and suppressed a second confession on the grounds that the original promise of hospitalization continued to influence him, making the second confession involuntary. The court wrote:

> There was additionally offered testimony by experts in the field of sign language for the deaf that the expression "Constitutional Rights," being an abstract idea, is extremely difficult to convey to the deaf, especially, as in this case, when the educational level of the individual is so curtailed. There

was testimony that the warning, "Do you understand that you have the right to have an attorney present at all times during the questioning?," may well have been signalled, and understood as "Do you understand it is *all right* to have an attorney present?," which obviously is far from the actual portent of the warning.[9]

Extra Jail Time

Without the assistance of an interpreter at the time of their arrest, deaf people often spend excessive time in jail, unaware of their right to counsel and to post bail; sometimes they are unaware even of the charges against them.

Oklahoma state law requires that

interpreters be provided to deaf defendants upon arrest. In one instance, however, a deaf man arrested for a misdemeanor was in jail for two days without being given an interpreter. In this case, the Oklahoma Supreme Court found that the state law applies to city police departments and that, because the deaf man could not understand his rights or communicate with those who could help him, he was forced to stay in jail longer than a hearing person would have.[10]

In another case, a deaf man remained in a St. Louis, Missouri, jail for five days after arrest without being provided an interpreter. The St. Louis police department had no written policy on the matter. The National Center for Law and the Deaf (NCLD) filed a complaint against the police department with the U.S. Department of Treasury Office of Revenue Sharing (ORS). The ORS had proposed Section 504 regulations requiring that agencies receiving revenue sharing funds "provide appropriate aids to individuals with impaired sensory, manual, or speaking skills, where necessary to afford such individuals equal opportunity to obtain the same result or to gain the same level of achievement as that provided to others."[11]

After an investigation by ORS, the police department issued a written policy stating that the arresting officer should decide when an interpreter would be provided. Because police officers dealing with deaf people fre-

quently try to get by with notewriting, ORS found this policy inadequate and directed the St. Louis police department to provide a qualified intepreter to any deaf person upon arrest and prior to interrogating or taking a statement. According to the directive, the interpreter should be appointed to serve throughout the arrest procedure in order to make certain that the deaf person is fully aware of the charges. The police department must also make known this policy to its officers by including a written directive in the department's procedure book. St. Louis's police department was required to take these steps or face a possible suspension of federal revenue sharing funds.

Qualified Interpreters

The Department of Justice's Section 504 regulation is specific in the requirements it makes of police departments receiving financial assistance:

> A recipient that employs fifteen or more persons shall provide appropriate auxiliary aids to qualified handicapped persons with impaired sensory, manual, or speaking skills where a refusal to make such provision would discriminatorily impair or exclude the participation of such persons in a program receiving Federal financial assistance. Such auxiliary aids may include . . . qualified interpreters. . . . Department officials may require recipients employing fewer than fifteen persons to provide auxiliary aids when this would not significantly impair the ability of the recipient to provide its benefits or services.[12]

The Justice Department's analysis of the regulation explains this requirement in more detail:

> Law enforcement agencies should provide for the availability of qualified interpreters (certified, where possible, by a recognized certification agency) to assist the agencies when dealing with hearing-impaired persons. Where the hearing-impaired person uses American Sign Language for communication, the term "qualified interpreter" would mean an interpreter skilled in communicating in American Sign Language. It is the responsibility of the law enforcement agency to determine whether the hearing-impaired person uses American Sign Language or Signed English to communicate.
>
> If a hearing-impaired person is arrested, the arresting officer's *Miranda* warning should be communicated to the arrestee on a printed form approved for such use by the law enforcement agency where there is no qualified interpreter immediately available and communication is otherwise inadequate. *The form should also advise the arrestee that the law enforcement agency has an obligation* under Federal law *to offer an interpreter* to the arrestee *without cost and that the agency will defer interrogation pending the appearance of an interpreter* (our emphasis).[13]

Neither the regulation nor its analysis limits the provision of interpreters to arrested hearing-impaired people. Victims and complainants are also entitled to them. In addition, hearing-impaired people who attend programs and functions sponsored by a law enforcement agency, such as informational workshops and educational programs, must be provided qualified interpreters upon request.

The analysis stresses the critical importance of the interpreter's qualifications. Quality can be ensured by contacting the local or state chapter of the Registry of Interpreters for the Deaf (RID) for a list of certified and qualified interpreters. If the interpreter is inadequate—as judged by either the hearing-impaired person, the interpreter, or a law enforcement or court official—another interpreter must be secured. The analysis places specific responsibility on the recipient agency to ascertain what kind of sign language the deaf person feels most comfortable with and then to secure an interpreter who is competent in that language.

Competence is Critical

Making the effort to secure a competent interpreter is critical. The existence of a federal or state law providing interpreters is in itself no guarantee that they are actually provided and that they function appropriately.

In Virginia, where state law requires the appointment of qualified interpreters, an unskilled and uncertified interpreter was provided to a deaf rape victim. Although the interpreter told the court that he was not skilled at reading sign language, the judge proceeded with the trial. When the prosecutor asked the victim what had happened, she gave the sign for "forced intercourse." The interpreter said that her reply was "made love," the sign for which is completely different. The legal effect of the intepreter's mistake was devastating because, in rape, force is the essential element. Later, when she answered, "blouse," to the prosecutor's question of what she was wearing, the interpreter told the court, "short blouse," creating the impression that she had dressed provocatively.[14]

Effective enforcement of the right to a qualified interpreter is extremely important. It will require a continuing effort to raise the awareness of judicial and administrative judges and court clerks about relevant laws and the communication patterns of deaf people.

The obligation of law enforcement agencies to provide interpreters is founded not only in regulation and statute but in constitutional law as well. Courts have suppressed evidence obtained from hearing-impaired defendants when it was found that the *Miranda* advice of rights was not adequately communicated.[15] In each case in which the confession was suppressed, the *Miranda* warning was conveyed in sign language beyond the defendant's level of comprehension.

Securing an interpreter with an RID legal skills certificate for a timely explanation of rights, accompanied by a careful explanation of every legal term and sign, is one way police departments can both prevent objections to the adequacy of the communication and comply with the Department of Justice's Section 504 regulations. Presentation of a printed advice of rights form without interpretation will seldom if ever be sufficient. Some police departments videotape all communications with hearing-impaired defendants in order to verify for the court that the rights warning was effectively communicated and that the interpreter acted properly.

Pre-Trial Preparation

The period between arrest, arraignment, and subsequent trial is critical for the defendant. A defense is formulated at this stage. Under the sixth amendment to the Constitution, every accused person has the right to have an attorney and to be effectively represented. In

DeRoche v. United States, the Court of Appeals for the Ninth Circuit held that effective assistance of counsel means adequate opportunity for the accused and his or her attorney to consult and prepare for arraignment and trial.[16] No attorney can effectively represent a client without a full understanding of the client's case. The Justice Department's Section 504 regulation requires that interpreters be provided to indigent deaf defendants for all phases of case preparation.[17] Interpreters also should be provided when, in preparation of pre-sentence or probation reports, it is necessary to interview a convicted deaf person. A Florida state judge used the authority of the Revenue Sharing Act and Section 504 of the Rehabilitation Act to convince a probation

officer to provide an interpreter to a deaf defendant.

Due Process and Access in Prison

Once in jail to serve their terms, deaf people are frequently denied basic due process rights and access to rehabilitation programs simply because prison staff cannot communicate with them. A deaf inmate of Maryland's prison system was denied an interpreter at a disciplinary hearing and was therefore unable to present a defense. The disciplinary board took away "good time" days that would have led to earlier release, and it transferred him for psychological evaluation from a minimum-security camp to a maximum-security house of corrections. The state psychologist there could not communicate with

him and, therefore, could not competently evaluate him.

The deaf man filed a lawsuit in federal district court in Baltimore requesting a court order requiring the state of Maryland to provide an interpreter to any deaf inmate who faces administrative charges. The suit argued that, without a qualified interpreter, a deaf inmate who depends on sign language cannot testify or question witnesses and is thereby denied his or her constitutional right to a fair hearing.

The federal judge approved a consent decree that provided interpreters for deaf prisoners in many situations of prison life: at adjustment team hearings; when officials give notice that a disciplinary report is being written; whenever a deaf inmate is provided counseling or psychiatric, psychological, or medical care; and in any on-the-job or vocational training or any educational program. This consent agreement is a model of how to provide deaf prisoners their basic due process rights and access to needed counseling, medical services, and rehabilitation programs.[18]

The Department of Justice's Section 504 regulation analysis specifically states that prisons

> Should provide for the availability of qualified interpreters (certified, where possible, by a recognized certification agency) to enable hearing-impaired inmates to participate on an equal basis with nonhandicapped inmates in the rehabilitation programs offered by the correctional agencies (e.g., educational programs).[19]

State Civil and Administrative Proceedings

In criminal proceedings, the constitutional rights to notice, confrontation, and effective assistance of counsel have compelled the right to an interpreter. Traditionally these rights have not been recognized as fundamental in civil proceedings, and many states lack statutes providing interpreters to deaf people in such settings.

However, the U.S. Supreme Court increasingly has required the observance of constitutional due process rights in certain civil proceedings and administrative hearings. These include juvenile hearings,[20] parole and probation revocation hearings,[21] prison disciplinary proceedings,[22] and passport reviews.[23]

In addition, the Department of Justice's analysis of its Section 504 regulation (quoted on page 119) specifically requires the appointment of interpreters in civil proceedings when the court system receives federal financial assistance. Section 504 can provide a remedy if the state or local government receives federal financial assistance from the Department of Treasury's Office of Revenue Sharing or other federal agencies.

Few states have laws providing interpreters for deaf people in administrative proceedings, which deal with matters such as worker's compensation, welfare, immigration, tax, licensing, school placement, employment disputes, and zoning hearings. These hearings affect many areas of our lives, and deaf citizens should neither be prevented from participating in them nor fail to get justice simply because a state refuses to provide interpreters.

Interpreter Privilege

States have begun to recognize that interpreters in a confidential attorney-client situation are covered by the attorney-client privilege. The privilege means that interpreters cannot be forced to reveal any information based on that confidential interview. The privilege exists to ensure that clients will freely discuss their problems with their lawyer without fear of disclosure. Kentucky, New Hampshire, Tennessee, and Virginia have laws explicitly applying this privilege to sign language interpreters.[24] In other states, laws and precedents pertaining to the status of translators should be applied also to sign language interpreters.

A Maryland circuit court ruled that interpreters could not be ordered to disclose statements that a deaf suspect made to his attorney. An interpreter with legal-specialist certification was subpoenaed to testify before a grand jury about a jailhouse interview between a deaf defendant, his attorney, and the defendant's relatives. The judge stated: "When both attorney and client depend on the use of an interpreter for communicating to one another, the interpreter serves as a vital link in the bond of the attorney-client relationship."[25] The judge also stated that the presence of close relatives at such interviews may be helpful in aiding the accuracy of the communication, thereby "enabling the attorney to provide meaningful assistance to his client."

The case was appealed. The Maryland Court of Special Appeals did not deal with the question of whether the communication was confidential. It reversed the decision saying that the lower court lacked the jurisdiction to issue the decree.[26]

Telephone Access

Section 504 regulations of each of the federal executive departments and the Office of Revenue Sharing require installation of telecommunication devices for deaf people (TDDs) in all federally assisted agencies with which the public has telephone contact. In the analysis of its regulation, the Justice Department refers specifically to the obligation of police departments:

> Law enforcement agencies are also required to install TTYs or equivalent mechanisms . . . to enable people with hearing and speaking impairments to communicate effectively with such agencies.[27]

The installation of TDDs at police stations can help protect the lives and property of hearing-impaired citizens. Moreover, the general public benefits from the ability of an additional segment of the local population to make police reports by telephone. Many cities across the country have already installed TDDs in their police departments and other offices.

Equal Justice

Although recent state and federal legislation has greatly advanced the rights of deaf people involved with the legal system, much remains to be done if they are to achieve full access and equal justice.

First, states without laws should adopt model statutes that provide qualified interpreters to any deaf party or witness in any judicial action.* In criminal cases, interpreters should be

*See Appendix D: "A Model Act to Provide for the Appointment of Interpreters for Hearing-Impaired Individuals for Administrative, Legislative, and Judicial Proceedings"

provided to the deaf person during any police interrogation. Civil and administrative proceedings should also require interpreters paid for by the government.

Second, laws such as the Rehabilitation Act of 1973 must be fully enforced. The Department of Justice must ensure full compliance with its regulation if the rights of deaf people involved with the legal system are to be protected.

Third, judges, court administrators, lawyers, and law enforcement officers must become more aware of the communication problems of deaf people.

Good laws, thorough enforcement, and enlightened attitudes will ensure that deaf people obtain equal justice under law.

Notes

1. Terry v. State of Alabama, 105 So. 386 (1925)

2. 28 *United States Code* §1827

3. 45 *Federal Register* 37,630 (1980)

4. Ibid.

5. Miranda v. Arizona, 384 U.S. 436 (1966)

6. M. Vernon, "Violation of Constitutional Rights: The Language-Impaired Person and the Miranda Warnings," *Journal of Rehabilitation of the Deaf* 11 (1978): 4.

7. Mary Furey, personal communication, June 1976

8. Vernon, "Violation of Constitutional Rights," p. 6

9. State of Maryland v. Barker, Crim. No.'s 17,995 and 19,518 (Md. Cir. Ct., Dec. 8, 1977)

10. Kiddy v. City of Oklahoma City, 576 P.2d 298 (S. Okla., 1978)

11. Section 51.55(c)(1) of Office of Revenue Sharing regulation to Section 122(a) of the State and Local Fiscal Assistance Act of 1972, as amended; 31 U.S.C. §1242(a)

12. 28 *Code of Federal Regulations* §42.503(f)

13. 28 C.F.R. §42, Subpart G

14. Commonwealth v. Edmonds, Cir. Ct. Staunton, Va. (1975)

15. See, for example, State of Maryland v. Barker (Note 9) and State of Oregon v. Mason, Crim. No. C-80-03-30821 (Ore. Cir. Ct., May 27, 1980)

16. 337 F.2d 606 (9th Cir. 1964)

17. 45 Fed. Reg. 37,630 (1980)

18. Pyles v. Kamka, Civil No. K-79-1864 (unreported decision), Feb. 20, 1980

19. 45 Fed. Reg. 37,630 (1980)

20. In Re Gault, 387 U.S. 1 (1967)

21. Wolff v. McDonnell, 418 U.S. 539 (1974)

22. Gagnon v. Scarpelli, 411 U.S. 778 (1973); and Morrissey v. Brewer, 408 U.S. 471 (1972)

23. Trop v. Dulles, 356 U.S. 86 (1958)

24. Kentucky Rev. Stat. §304.064 (Supp. 1976); New Hampshire H.B. 870, Ch. 521.1–521.5 (1977); Tennessee Code Ann. §24-108; and Virginia Code Ann. §2.1-560 through 2.1-563, §19.2-164, §8.01-400.1, and §63.1-85.4

25. Touhey v. Duckett, 19 Crim. L. Rptr. 2483 (Cir. Ct. Anne Arundel County, Md., 1976)

26. Duckett v. Touhey, 36 Md. App. 238 (1977)

27. 45 Fed. Reg. 37,630 (1980)

CHAPTER TEN
Television

Deaf people receive information through what they see. Television, therefore, would seem to be an ideal medium. But most televised information is still presented in the form of sound. The content of the communication is therefore largely inaccessible to deaf people.

Recent advances in technology, however, enable deaf people to benefit fully from television. These include captioning of programs and emergency bulletins, public service programs produced especially for the deaf audience, sign language newscasts, and new electronic systems to aid in presenting visual information. In addition, recent Federal Communications Commission (FCC) rulings require broadcasters to consider the deaf community's needs when preparing their programming. Each of these developments will be examined here in light of how they increase television's potential for deaf people.

Emergency Captioning

Before 1977, when the FCC adopted a rule requiring television broadcasters to present emergency bulletins in visual as well as oral form, deaf people faced danger because they could not hear televised disaster warnings.[1] In an emergency the television station would interrupt the sound portion of the signal to make oral announcements, but the picture would continue without any indication that something was wrong. Sometimes "Emergency Bulletin" would appear on the screen, and an off-camera announcer would read the details of the emergency. The deaf viewer, unable to hear what was said, could not make realistic plans for safety.

When fires ravaged wide sections of California in 1970, officials used loudspeakers and radio and television to warn residents to evacuate threatened areas. Several hearing-impaired people burned to death, however, because they could not hear the loudspeakers or the radio bulletins and because the television announcements gave no visual information about the danger. Their

deaths could have been prevented except for simple thoughtlessness.

This and similar tragedies prompted appeals to the FCC. Thousands of letters from people all over the country convinced the FCC to adopt a visual warning rule. The "Operation During Emergency" section states:

> Any emergency information transmitted in accordance with this Section shall be transmitted both aurally and visually or only visually. Television broadcast stations may use any method of visual presentation which results in a legible message conveying the essential information. Methods which may be used include but are not limited to slides, electronic captioning, manual methods (e.g., hand printing) or mechanical printing processes. However, when emergency operation is being conducted under a National, State, or Local Level Emergency Broadcast System (EBS) Plan, emergency announcements shall be transmitted both aurally and visually.[2]

Under the Communications Act of 1934, the FCC is authorized to make such rules to protect the safety of life and property through the use of electronic media and to improve the quality of those media in ways that promote the public interest.[3]

Even though the visual warning rule has been in effect for several years, many television stations still do not comply. A person should contact the station and explain to the station manager the need for the visual emergency bulletin, citing the above FCC rule. If the station still refuses to provide vi-

sual emergency warnings, then a person can file a complaint with the FCC. Complaints are considered when a station applies to renew its FCC license.

The Growth of Captioning

Captioning of regular newscasts and educational and entertainment programs has been a major advance in making television more accessible to hearing-impaired people. Captioning takes two forms: (1) open captioning involves the broadcast of captions on a regular television signal transmitted to all receivers; (2) closed captioning involves transmission of the caption on a special television signal that requires use of a decoder-adapter on the TV receiver. The captions appear only on the modified receivers. Some people think closed captioning is preferable since it does not distract the hearing audience.

The Public Broadcasting Service (PBS), a nonprofit network with about 250 noncommercial television stations in the U.S., is very active in the field of captioning. Boston's WGBH was the first PBS station to use open captions. In December 1973 WGBH began captioning the half-hour "ABC Evening News," a task that daily took five staff people five hours to complete. Because news programs are faster paced than other kinds of programs, the text had to be reduced and the language simplified, often resulting in the loss of some information. But open captioning was an important interim measure in making television more accessible to all hearing-impaired people.

The PBS network began working on a closed captioning system in 1972. In 1975 it filed a petition with the FCC to reserve a segment of the television signal known as "line 21" for transmission of caption material.[4] The deaf community supported the idea. Commercial networks opposed it, saying that deaf people do not watch television and would not buy the special decoders.

The FCC accepted the PBS petition in 1976 and reserved line 21 for closed captions. With HEW funding, PBS developed a closed caption system for its own network use. In 1980 Sears, Roebuck, and Co. was contracted to manufacture the decoders, called TeleCaption units. The decoders cost approximately $260 and can be bought through the Sears mail-order catalogue or from any Sears retail store. Sears also sells television sets with built-in decoders. The nineteen-inch color sets sell for $530, about $100 more than the same model without the decoder. Approximately 35,000 decoders had been purchased by mid-1981.

The National Captioning Institute (NCI) was established in 1979 as an independent, nonprofit company to do closed captioning of television programs. With each purchase of a decoder from Sears, eight dollars of the purchase price goes to NCI to allow it to caption more programs. The institute has two captioning centers, in Los Angeles, California, and Falls Church, Virginia. Its services are available to local stations, networks, and independent producers at a cost of $2,200 for each one-hour captioned program.

The PBS, NBC, and ABC networks together provided about 22 hours per week of captioned prime-time programming in 1980. The number of hours is expected to increase as more consumers start using decoders.

Ascertainment of Needs

The FCC requires television broadcasters to ascertain and respond to the problems, needs, and interests of the community in which they are licensed. They must consult community leaders who represent nineteen institutions and groups listed on FCC's "Community Ascertainment Checklist."[5] Broadcasters must then plan programming that responds to the needs identified by these community leaders.

Disabled people are not specifically included among these nineteen categories. While a general category called "Other" exists, broadcasters are not required to seek out any particular other group to determine its needs. The FCC amended its rules in 1980, however, to allow a group representing a particular segment of the community not represented on the checklist to inform the broadcaster about its needs.[6] The broadcaster then determines whether this group is "significant" in the community. If so, then the station must respond to the group's needs and con-

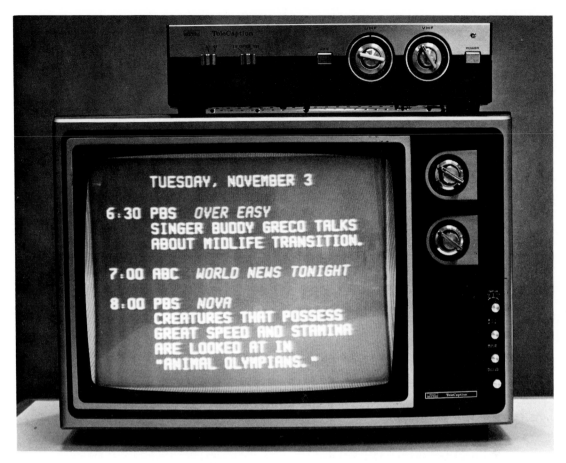

TUESDAY, NOVEMBER 3

6:30 PBS OVER EASY
          SINGER BUDDY GRECO TALKS
          ABOUT MIDLIFE TRANSITION.

7:00 ABC WORLD NEWS TONIGHT

8:00 PBS NOVA
          CREATURES THAT POSSESS
          GREAT SPEED AND STAMINA
          ARE LOOKED AT IN
          "ANIMAL OLYMPIANS."

tinue to contact its representatives as long as the group remains significant. "Significance" is determined by the total number of people making up the community segment, its influence, and the distinct nature of its needs.

This amendment of the FCC's "ascertainment-of-needs" requirement opens the door for hearing-impaired people to influence television programming. Their large numbers and the distinct character of their special needs make them a significant group.

Broadcaster Compliance

In 1983 the U.S. Supreme Court ruled that the FCC, in its licensing proceedings, is not required by Section 504 of the Rehabilitation Act to evaluate a public television station's service to hearing-impaired viewers by a stronger standard than that applicable to commercial stations.[7] The Court held that Congress left initial enforcement of Section 504 violations to the federal agency that gives money to public television stations—something the FCC does not do. If a licensee should be found in violation of Section 504, however, the FCC must consider such a violation in determining that station's license renewal.

The case arose when Sue Gottfried, a Los Angeles woman with a hearing loss, asked the FCC to deny renewal of the licenses of eight Los Angeles television stations—seven commercial and one public—because their programming was not accessible to hearing-impaired people.

A U.S. Court of Appeals had upheld the FCC's license renewal to the seven commercial stations but had required the FCC to hold a public hearing before acting on license renewal for public television station KCET-TV.[8] Because public television stations receive federal financial assistance, the appeals court stated that they have a legal duty under Section 504 to provide service to disabled persons. The purpose of the public hearing would be to find out what efforts KCET-TV had made to meet the programming needs of hearing-impaired people and if these were good faith efforts to comply with Section 504.

The Supreme Court recognized that "the interest in having all television stations—public and commercial—consider and serve their handicapped viewers is equally strong." But the Court concluded that, until Congress or the FCC requires a stronger public interest standard for public television stations than for commercial stations, the FCC

can decline to impose a greater obligation on the public stations to provide special programming for hearing-impaired people.

Two dissenting justices agreed with the appeals court decision that Section 504 required the FCC not to renew the public television station's license until the FCC had investigated and accepted the station's efforts to meet the programming needs of hearing-impaired people.

Full Television Access

The public interest responsibility of television broadcasters is not limited to an audience with normal hearing. Technological advances have produced the necessary equipment to enable deaf people to have meaningful access to television.

Continued support from the federal government, changing attitudes within the broadcast industry, and persistent action by the community could make television fully accessible for many more deaf people.

Notes

1. FCC Docket No. 20,659, RM 2502 (1977)

2. 47 *Code of Federal Regulations* §73.1250(h)

3. 47 *United States Code* §151 *et seq.*

4. FCC Docket No. 20,793, RM 2616 (1975)

5. FCC BC Docket No. 78-237, RM 2937 (1980)

6. Ibid.

7. Community Television of Southern California v. Gottfried, 103 S. Ct. 885 (1983)

8. FCC v. Gottfried, 655 F.2d 297 (D.C. Cir 1981)

CHAPTER ELEVEN
Telephone Service

Society has isolated deaf people for centuries. Today such exclusion is perhaps most obvious in the telecommunications system. Rapid and efficient telecommunications services, readily available to almost all hearing Americans, are largely denied to those who cannot hear. As currently set up, the system places unnecessary barriers of expense and difficulty on deaf people, limiting their ability to communicate with family, friends, businesses, government, and social services. For deaf people to participate fully in our society, telecommunications must be made as rapid, efficient, and reasonably priced for people who cannot hear as it is for those who can.

For the past several years, hearing-impaired people have tried to get equal access to telecommunications services by working with federal and state legislative bodies and regulatory agencies. Four major goals have been

- Rate reduction for long-distance TDD calls;

- Improved customer services;
- Telephone equipment—price and availability; and
- Telephones that are compatible with hearing aids.

Most of the proceedings have dealt with TDD-equipped telephones.* A person using a TDD can communicate by telephone only with other people who have them. Because few telephone companies provide them for customers, TDDs must be purchased commercially. The TDDs and the acoustic coupling devices they require cost between $200 and $1,000, depending on the type of machine and its features. A limited number of retired and converted teletype machines are donated to deaf people and organizations by telephone and telegraph companies.

---

*See page 7 for an explanation of TDD terminology and equipment.

Regulation of Telecommunication

Telephone companies are public utilities whose rates and practices are regulated by federal and state agencies. The federal agency that regulates interstate telephone rates and practices is the Federal Communication Commission (FCC). Each state has its own agency with power to regulate the operations of telephone companies within the state (intrastate). The state agencies are usually called public utility commissions (PUCs) or public service commissions. The FCC was established by Congress and the PUCs by the state legislatures to ensure that telephone companies operate in the public interest, i.e., that they provide adequate service to the public for a fair price and that they comply with applicable laws and regulations.

The agencies set the rates that the companies can charge. They allow the companies enough revenue to operate, provide the service, and make a reasonable profit. The company must justify the rates it wants at a public hearing. It gives the FCC or the state PUC detailed financial information about its expenses and equipment. Consumers and other interested people can participate in the hearings. They can tell the agencies

about the services they need and the rates they consider fair. The final decision about the rate, or "tariff," is made by the FCC or the PUC.

Long-Distance Rate Reduction

The charge for a long-distance call is usually based on the number of minutes the telephone line is used, the distance between the callers, and the day and time of day the call is placed. Because TDD calls take much longer than voice calls to communicate the same message, long-distance TDD calls are very expensive.

Although TDDs can transmit at a maximum speed of sixty words per minute, most TDD calls are transmitted at a much slower rate. One reason is that some deaf people have below-average skills with written as well as spoken English vocabulary and syntax. The language they are most comfortable with is American Sign Language (ASL). They communicate in English more slowly than they communicate in sign language. Even among skilled English-language users, only a small percentage can type sixty words per minute. By contrast, the estimated average speaking rate for native users of American English is 165 words per minute. Thus a typical TDD user pays $6.50 to have the same long-distance telephone conversation that a hearing person could have for only $2.50.

In 1977 the National Center for Law

and the Deaf petitioned the FCC to begin a formal inquiry into the telecommunications needs of deaf people.[1] Many deaf organizations and individuals submitted written comments to the FCC on the kinds of telephone service they need and why they need them.

In August 1981 the American Telephone and Telegraph Company (AT&T) petitioned the FCC for reduction of interstate long-distance rates for hearing-impaired TDD customers. The FCC approved the petition and the rates went into effect in November 1981.[2] Rates were reduced 35 percent for daytime and 60 percent for nighttime calls. Late night and weekend rates remained the same. The new interstate rates applied only to certified hearing-impaired TDD users who dial direct and who call from and are billed to their residence.

The first qualification—"certified hearing-impaired TDD users"—created a problem for some deaf people. The new rates automatically applied to hearing-impaired people already certified for reductions in intrastate TDD rates. But some states had not yet reduced intrastate TDD rates and therefore had no certification process. Some other states had certified hearing as well as hearing-impaired TDD users for the intrastate reduction. Some hearing-impaired customers, therefore, had to be either certified or recertified in order to qualify for the interstate reduction.

Deaf customers have used two means to request rate reductions for intrastate long-distance calls. In some states they have petitioned the state PUC for a rate reduction and presented evidence at an administrative PUC hearing about the need for it. In other states they have asked the legislature to pass a law requiring the state PUC to adopt the rate reduction. The choice between these two approaches depends on where deaf customers have the best contacts and most influence and whether or not the state PUC is willing to grant a reduction without specific authority from the state legislature.

Intrastate long-distance rates have been reduced by a certain percentage in some states. For example, Connecticut ordered its TDD rates reduced by 75 percent in 1977. In Kentucky and Tennessee, intrastate long-distance TDD calls made during the day are billed at evening rates and evening calls at the night and weekend rates. There is no additional discount for calls made during night and weekend times. New York Telephone Company has a unique discount system: A 25-percent across-the-board reduction for local service as well as intrastate long-distance phone calls is given to any household with a certified hearing-impaired resident.

A wide variety of methods has been adopted by states and telephone companies to administer these rate changes. Some states, such as New York, require deaf customers to submit a statement from a doctor, audiologist, or public agency certifying that they are hearing-impaired. Other states merely ask deaf customers to apply for the reduced rate, without requiring certification. New York's reduction applies to the deaf person's entire household. In other states, reductions apply only to calls made with a TDD; if a household has hearing as well as deaf residents, TDD calls are charged separately from the voice calls.

Value of Service

The primary argument in favor of a rate reduction is that charges should be based on the value of the service to the customer rather than on the cost to the telephone company of providing the service. The value of a call made by a TDD user is exactly the same as the value of the same call made by a hearing person, yet the charge for the TDD call is more than double, even after the November 1981 rate reductions.

Some state PUCs have ruled that rates should be reduced for TDD users because of public policy considerations. The telephone system is supposed to provide universal communication services at fair and reasonable rates. If homes in rural or mountainous areas were charged the actual cost to the telephone company of running telephone lines and installing equipment, their rates would be very high. Yet all residential telephone customers, urban or rural, are charged the same fee for basic telephone service. Why? Because the value of that service is the same for everyone, and because the telephone system is more useful for everyone if it reaches as many people as possible.

The cost of providing service to all households is averaged, and the cost is spread among all customers. It is in the public interest to make sure that deaf people have access to the telephone system on the same basis as other telephone users.

Customer Services

Deaf telephone subscribers pay for but generally cannot make use of a sub-stantial number of telephone customer services, including operator, directory, and telephone business office assistance. Many types of calls, such as emergency, person-to-person, and collect long-distance calls, require operator assistance. Directory assistance is necessary for new listings and for long-distance and other calls for which no telephone directory is available. When people desire telephone repairs or

installations or have questions about telephone bills, they must call the telephone business office.

In 1980 AT&T, which operates the Bell System telephone companies, initiated a nationwide TDD-operator system. This system uses one national toll-free number, 1-800-855-1155, and regional TDD operators. These operators help TDD users place long-distance collect, person-to-person, coin phone, credit card, and third-party calls. The TDD operator also provides the same directory assistance services that are available to hearing customers. One serious shortcoming, however, is that the operator does not have a directory of TDD numbers and conventional telephone directories do not note all phones having TDD capability.

While the nationwide system is very useful, it may not be sufficient to meet all the customer service needs of deaf people. The TDD operator assistance is provided by AT&T to all TDD customers, whether they are local customers of an affiliated Bell company or of an independent telephone company. But deaf customers of independent companies may find that the system does not provide adequate access to a company's business office, repair services, or directory listings. The TDD operator at AT&T must relay calls to these offices, which often do not have TDD equipment. Without such equipment, the essential services offered by the company are unusable.

Unresolved Issues

Other customer service issues have not been resolved by the new TDD operator system. For example, recorded "intercept" messages are used when a customer dials a telephone number that has been changed, disconnected, or for some other reason is not functioning. These messages do not register with TDD equipment. When TDD users encounter a recorded message, they know their call has not been completed but do not know why. They either wait on the line for extended periods or continue trying to reach the number, even though it is not in service.

Deaf advocacy groups have only recently raised this issue and sought to require that routine recorded messages be encoded for TDD users. Telephone companies have opposed the proposal, arguing that it is technologically difficult and prohibitively expensive.

Telephone companies should be required to provide all of these services to TDD users because the services are basic and indispensible. Deaf customers should receive basic services because they pay for and need them the same as hearing customers.

Deaf customers may need certain special customer services not offered to the general subscriber. For example, a customer may need to indicate in the telephone directory that a particular phone number is only TDD-equipped or that it can be answered by voice or TDD. Most telephone companies charge a monthly fee for such "additional lines of information." In some regions, emergency TDD numbers are not included in the emergency listings on page one of telephone directories.

It is not unreasonable to request some accommodation from telephone companies. However, the legal definition of what a company must provide its customers is changing rapidly. It is important, therefore, that deaf advocates obtain advice of a knowledgeable attorney before making formal requests of the FCC or state PUCs.

Phone Company-Supplied Equipment

TDD-Equipped Pay Telephones.
Public telephones have an important communication function. Deaf people who cannot afford their own telephones or TDDs or who are away from home need to use pay phones. Since few TDDs are portable, most TDD users are unable to use conventional pay phones. Many advocacy groups for hearing- and speech-impaired people would like to require telephone companies to provide a reasonable number of TDD-equipped pay telephones in public places. Those now in existence are widely used.

Strategic and accessible locations for public telephones include airports, shopping malls, train stations, public libraries, hospitals, police stations, and other public buildings. Telephones that are TDD-equipped must be located in sheltered places to protect them from weather damage or vandalism. Properly secured, they are no more susceptible to vandalism than regular telephones.

Elimination of Charges for Special Equipment.
Hearing-impaired people use a variety of special adaptive devices on telephones. They rely on flashing light relays, special tone ringers, fans, or similar devices instead of the usual phone bell to alert them to incoming calls. When using the phone, many people require amplifier switches on their receivers that boost sounds to audible levels. But not all telephone companies provide hearing-impaired customers with the special equipment they need to make conventional telephones usable. When a telephone company does provide such equipment, it often charges high rates for installation and use.

Hearing telephone customers do not pay an additional charge for the bells on their telephones. But deaf people are usually required to pay installation fees plus additional monthly charges for flashing lights or similar devices that serve the same function as a bell and that are not necessarily more expensive. Many deaf people and groups believe this is unfair and argue that such equipment should be available without additional charge to any telephone customer who needs it. Special devices needed to make a telephone usable should be included in the basic monthly service charge paid by all telephone users.

Telephone companies argue that the special equipment entails extra expenses and that the people who require them should pay for them. The counter-argument is that there must be a substantial difference in function, service, or conditions to justify differences in rates. Since there is clearly no substantial difference in functon, deaf customers should not have to pay charges for them in addition to what they pay for basic telephone service. In addition, some of the special adaptive devices are no more expensive than standard equipment.

In 1979 AT&T issued a policy statement to its operating companies concerning prices of terminal equipment for disabled people. The policy seeks to price those products designed primarily for disabled people so that the company makes no profit on them. Since

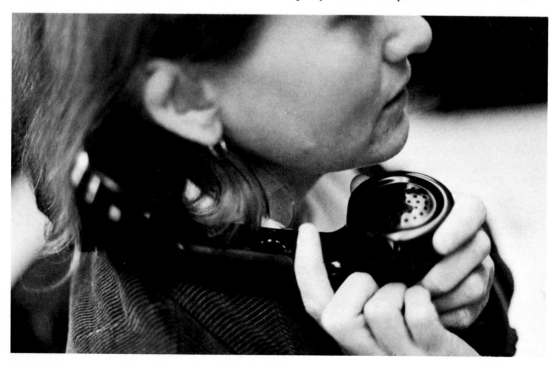

rates and tariffs for such equipment must be approved by state regulatory agencies, the policy statement itself does not actually change any prices. However, it does provide guidance to affiliated companies on services used by disabled people.

Phone Company-Supplied TDDs. The costs of owning a TDD can be prohibitive for deaf people, most of whom have below-average incomes. In addition to the initial cost, the TDD user must also pay for repair, maintenance, and, if needed, paper supplies. Expense is the main reason that only about 40,000 TDDs are in use today in the United States.

Many deaf groups believe that telephone companies should be required to furnish and maintain TDD equipment for all deaf, hearing-impaired, and speech-impaired customers who need it, just as they supply necessary telephone equipment to hearing customers.

Only a few telephone companies now offer TDDs for rental. Rental fees can be very high. In Texas, for example, the charge was $25.00 per month for AT&T customers in September 1980. In a few states, lower rates have been adopted by state PUCs. Illinois Bell was offering a TDD for rental at $14.00 per month to customers certified as deaf. This price was designed to reflect the actual cost to the telephone company of supplying the device, without any contribution to the telephone company's profits or general administrative expenses. Hearing customers rent-

ing a TDD from Illinois Bell were charged $30.50 per month.

The most dramatic development to date occurred in California in 1979. The state legislature ordered all telephone companies to supply TDDs to deaf customers as part of the basic local service—without additional charge. The state PUC was given four years to implement this plan fully. It must hold hearings to determine the type of equipment to be offered, the criteria for eligibility, and where the plan should first be implemented.

California's TDD plan raises a major new concern: The plan could effectively mandate and promote the use of archaic technology. As mentioned, TDDs are fairly new devices. Research and development is advancing rapidly. One promising advance is an eight-level code called ASCII (American Standard Code Information Interaction). New ASCII-coded TDDs can "talk" with computers and transmit faster than conventional TDDs, thus requiring less time and money to complete a call.

The problem with the new code is that today's conventional TDDs use an incompatible code—the Baudot code—and conversion to the new system would be very expensive. People who have Baudot TDDs would not be able to "talk" with people using the new ASCII machines. They would eventually have to replace their Baudot machines. Dual capacity TDDs—those that could switch from Baudot to ASCII and back—are now being developed. When dual-capacity TDDs become generally available, it will be a giant and timely step forward in effective telecommunication for deaf people.

In the meantime, telephone companies that are now required to supply TDDs will saturate their markets with equipment that soon will be obsolete. If a company is required to furnish a TDD to a deaf customer now, the company may feel little or no obligation to replace it with a more advanced model within a few years. Many deaf advocacy groups have considered this policy dilemma and decided to wait until dual-capacity TDDs become available before requesting telephone company-provided TDDs.

Another concern arises from an FCC decision on April 7, 1980. In a proceeding called the "Second Computer Inquiry," the FCC deregulated the sale of terminal equipment, including telephones.[3] In the near future the sale of such equipment will no longer be regulated by government agencies. The equipment will be available on the open market from any company that chooses to offer equipment for sale or lease.

Telephone "basic service" traditionally has been defined as provision of a basic black phone and connection to transmission lines and the telephone network. Under the FCC ruling, "basic service" has been redefined to mean only connection to transmission lines. Other services are considered to be "enhanced" and are not subject to regu-

lation under Title II of the Communications Act. Equipment that a customer installs at home will now be available only on the commercial market. This complicates the situation for advocates of the hearing-impaired who believe that telephone companies should supply TDDs as part of their "basic service." The full implications of this decision for deaf customers are not yet clear.

Hearing Aid Compatibility

Half of the hearing aids in use in the United States are "telephone switch." A lever on the device allows the hearing aid to pick up sound waves generated by the electromagnetic field of the telephone receiver. The device is useless unless the telephone has a certain amount of electromagnetic leakage. Telephones with the required leakage are considered to be compatible with these hearing aids.

Most telephones manufactured in this country until recently had strong electromagnetic fields, but newer phones and phones manufactured abroad and by independent telephone companies lack the necessary leakage. Few compatible telephones will be in use in ten years at current rates of replacement. Many people believe that something must be done to ensure that all hearing-impaired people can use all telephones or at least know of and have access to ones they can use.

The telephone industry has voluntarily agreed to make public telephones compatible with hearing aids. The companies are in the process of replacing all incompatible pay phone receivers with compatible ones. The latter can be identified by a blue grommet (rubber or plastic tube) where the telephone cord is connected to the receiver. If the phone has no grommet or has a black grommet, it is not compatible with "telephone switch" hearing aids.

Maryland has passed legislation requiring all public telephones to be compatible with hearing aids and requiring the telephone company to inform customers about compatible models when they order telephone equipment. The state PUC has also started a program of replacing all incompatible telephones in Maryland hospitals.

The Organization for Use of the Telephone (OUT) has been successful in getting legislation introduced in Congress which would require all telephones sold, rented, or manufactured in the United States to be compatible with hearing aids.[4] Hearings on the bill were held in 1980, and the bill was reintroduced in 1981.[5]

New Developments

Telephone accessibility is extremely important for hearing-impaired people. Lack of access to the telephone system dramatically increases their isolation. This chapter provides only a summary of the major issues and some of the approaches that advocates of the hearing-impaired have taken.

There are many strategic and legal factors to consider before initiating a formal proceeding before the FCC or a state PUC. These considerations are complicated by the dramatic changes in telephone technology and service expected in the next few years. New devices will become available which will provide better and cheaper communication for deaf people. New methods of providing services and competition in the telephone manufacturing and service industry will alter the service rates and equipment prices. The role of regulatory agencies will also change. Deaf people and their advocates should become knowledgeable about these telecommunication developments in order to be prepared to take advantage of changes when they occur.

Notes

1. FCC Docket 78-50

2. FCC Transmittal No. 13,822 (August 1981)

3. FCC Docket 20,828, FCC 80-189, 45 *Federal Register* 31,319 (May 13, 1980)

4. For more information about compatibility issues, contact OUT, Box 175, Owings Mill, MD 21117. Telephone (301) 655-1827.

5. H.R. 375 and S. 604 (1981)

CHAPTER TWELVE
State Legislatures and Commissions

Since the 1980 elections, the federal government has sought to cut drastically both the budgets and the regulations for numerous programs that have assisted the poor and other minority groups, including the disabled. The policy of the Reagan administration has been to reduce the role of the federal government and to funnel lump sums of less money to the state governments. The states thus have a larger role in funding and regulating— or deciding not to fund or regulate— such programs.

One result of this policy is that hearing-impaired people and their advocates must increasingly turn to state governments to provide not only services but access to those services. This requires increased awareness of the state legislative process and of the purposes that can be served by state commissions. Those two factors are the substance of this chapter. First, however, there is a true story about the patience and persistence required to get

one state government to approve a bill benefitting hearing-impaired people.

Maryland enacted legislation in 1980 establishing an outpatient mental health program for deaf people. The requirements for staff expertise are spelled out in the law: Staff must be fluent in receptive and expressive sign language, including American Sign Language, or become so within one year of being employed. The professional staff must have experience in assessment techniques, individual psychotherapy, and group psychotherapy with hearing-impaired people. They must also have practical knowledge of deaf psychology.

The problems of hearing-impaired people under treatment in Maryland's mental health facilities were first brought to light by psychologist Allen Sussman in a presentation at the 1977 convention of the Maryland Association of the Deaf (MAD). Sussman pointed out that several deaf persons in Maryland hospitals were largely being neglected because there was no regular staff trained in aspects of deafness or fluent in sign language. The association responded by establishing a task force to meet formally with officials of the Maryland Department of Health and Mental Hygiene (DHMH) to discuss the problems and suggested solutions. The department responded to the proposed solutions by saying that it lacked money to pay for the specialized mental health services that hearing-impaired patients needed.

Members and officials of MAD worked with the staff of the National Center for Law and the Deaf (NCLD) to develop a legal strategy. They concluded that litigation would be expensive, time consuming, and probably not result in the needed services.

The Story of One Bill

A legislative approach was adopted, with MAD and NCLD working closely to draft a bill. Delegate Raymond Beck sponsored the bill in the Maryland House of Delegates, and DHMH supported the legislation. After hearings that committee chairperson Torrey Brown characterized as among the better ones he had seen in his years in the general assembly, the bill passed quickly in the house but got stuck in the senate's finance committee. Late in the legislative session, confusion arose in committee hearings over the composition of the proposed advisory committee and the statutory definition of who is eligible for the proposed ser-

vice. Amendments were made which required house approval.

Bill supporters were frustrated and disappointed when the 1979 legislative session expired with no action on the bill. They regrouped before the next session and resolved all differences of opinion about the definition of a person qualified for the service and about the composition of the advisory committee. They sought bipartisan support, and identical bills were introduced simultaneously in both the house and the senate to speed action. The agreed-upon definition of an eligible person was "an individual whose hearing impairment is so severe that the individual is impaired in processing linguistic information through hearing, with or without amplification."

The measure was one of the first introduced in the 1980 session and, backed by the organized and demonstrated support of the deaf community, passed both houses quickly. Governor Harry Hughes received a large delegation of deaf people in the capitol and, on May 6, 1980, signed the bill.[1]

Seven months later, however, the governor indicated that he would cut funding for the new program because of budgetary problems. A coalition of deaf organizations quickly responded by meeting with the governor and organizing a rally which helped convince the governor not to cut the program. The outpatient program is now operating at Family Service of Prince George's County, Maryland.

Lobbying in Your State Legislature

The above account points out some of the triumphs and frustrations of the state legislative process. Attention to organization, timing, and detail are important before, during, and after a bill is processed. All of these factors are discussed in more detail in the following guide to working effectively with state governors and legislators.[2]

Preparing for Action

1. State organizations of and for hearing-impaired people must set priorities. What specific services or protections do deaf citizens of your state need most?

2. Concentrate on these basic goals.

3. Can you achieve your goals through state agencies and the governor's office without legislative action, or do you need a state law?

4. Develop contacts with the heads of state agencies and find out if there are existing funds in the state agency to provide the services you need. Work with the governor's staff on the possibility of the governor issuing an executive order to provide you the protection you want. In Virginia the head of the state human resources agency required all state agencies and institutions to pay for qualified interpreters for deaf citizens seeking access to their services. In Illinois the governor issued an executive order to require interpreters, when requested, at all state meetings and conferences.

5. If you need a state law, first try to get support from the state agency that would administer the program. Encourage them to recommend to the governor that your proposal be included in their budget.

6. If the agency refuses, work directly with the governor's staff to include your priority in the governor's budget. In most states, legislators approve most of the governor's budget. The governor's full-time, professional staff and the state agency personnel have the data and expertise that often persuade part-time legislators with limited staff. Legislators will more often support, amend, or reject the governor's budget items than initiate their own proposals. If you try to approach a legislator directly and independently, the executive branch may oppose your proposal. Even if the governor's staff considers your proposal worthwhile, they may oppose it because it upsets the governor's budget. This is especially true given tough economic times and the pressure for balanced budgets.

7. Sometimes the governor will not agree to support your proposal. Do not give up! Seek out influential legislators who are sympathetic to your goal. Try to get them to introduce a bill.

8. One big plus is to get a legislator—preferably one who sits on the committee that will hear the bill—to sponsor your bill. A legislator who knows the committee members well is

best situated to move your bill through the committee.

9. Before you and other bill supporters meet with your legislative sponsor(s), *work out your differences.* It is important for leaders of all state organizations of and for hearing-impaired people to meet and agree on all parts of the bill before it is filed. Too often some organizations have not been consulted or involved in planning a bill because of philosophical, political, or personality differences. After a bill is introduced, these organizations sometimes object to parts of the bill due to misunderstanding the bill's purpose or because of major or minor errors or omissions. These objections create confusion in legislators' minds and lead to delay, withdrawal, or defeat of a bill. It is imperative that a united front be presented to the legislators.

10. *Do your homework.* Gather facts on why the bill is needed. Document with actual experiences. The most important question the legislators will want answered is "how much will the bill cost the taxpayers?" Advocates for the hearing-impaired in North Carolina effectively answered this question in support of a comprehensive interpreter bill. First they compiled the number of times interpreters were used in court cases county-by-county; then they multiplied by the standard state interpreter fee for the hours involved. They calculated the actual costs for interpreters paid out by interpreter referral agencies. Data were also collected from

other states that had state funds available for interpreter services; this showed the costs per year for providing interpreters in criminal, civil, and administrative proceedings.

Such detailed information should be provided to the legislative office that develops the fiscal note (calculates the annual cost of implementing the bill). These offices frequently have no idea how to estimate the fiscal cost for interpreters. Any hard data you can provide them, especially if they total a low but realistic figure, can help sway votes to support your bill. Also, find out how many hearing-impaired people in the state could benefit from the law. Will it help people throughout the state or only in one or two counties or cities? Collect data on how often the service will be needed. For example, if you want an interpreter bill to cover civil proceedings, how many cases were there in the state last year in which a deaf person requested interpreter services for a civil trial (such as a car accident case)?

11. When you meet with your legislative sponsor, present him/her with as complete a bill as possible, including your supporting research. The state legislator will frequently have limited time and staff resources. Your sponsor can help on the bill's wording and will refer the bill to the legislative drafting office for a final draft that meets all legal requirements. Urge your sponsor to prefile the bill if possible that year. Prefiling helps ensure an early hearing on

your bill and gives you time before the legislative session begins to sign up cosponsors. Having both Democrat and Republican sponsors is helpful.

12. If a state legislature meets only for a few months, try to arrange for sponsors in both the house and senate to introduce identical bills. This will ensure hearings in both houses and a legislative advocate for your bill in each chamber.

13. Form coalitions with other organizations with similar interests. Coalitions give you clout with both the legislators and the governor. Senior citizen organizations are very powerful in many states due to their experience, their high voter turnout, and their

invaluable time to lobby. They are an ally worth cultivating. Many of their interests coincide with yours. Parents' groups and professionals working for hearing-impaired children and adults should be part of your network. Finally, develop ties with organizations representing other disabilities and work together on common objectives. Coalitions are needed throughout the legislative process to ensure passage and implementation of needed laws and services.

When the Legislative Session Begins

1. The most crucial step in the legislative process is getting your bill re-

ported favorably out of committee. The house and senate usually support a bill approved by a committee. If a committee votes down your bill, getting the full house or senate to vote on it is very difficult. In Maryland, for example, a bill rejected by a committee can be brought to a floor vote only by petition of three senators or fifteen delegates. A bill frequently is amended or killed in committee. You must, therefore, devote considerable effort to

- presenting persuasive testimony,
- having answers for committee members, and
- demonstrating wide support for the bill through speakers representing different groups and by having many supporters at the hearing.

The job of persuasion must continue after the hearing.

2. Encourage letter writing to members of the committee and individual lobbying with legislators. An individualized letter discussing a relevant personal experience from a person in the legislator's home district is most effective. Try to organize a network of people in your state who can be mobilized quickly before the vote on your bill.

3. Remember that a legislator's time is valuable. You are competing with people who lobby for a living. You must be prepared on short notice to meet a legislator and explain concisely why your bill is needed.

4. Try to avoid amendments of your bill in the second chamber that considers it. If the senate amends a bill that passed the house, the amended bill must go back to the house for approval. There may not be time left for a house vote. A sad example of this procedure occurred in the Maryland General Assembly in 1979; as described early in this chapter, an amended bill to set up an outpatient mental health program died when time ran out.

5. Compromise is often necessary to gain passage and the governor's approval. Remembering your basic goal, however, you should staunchly resist amendments that cut funds, staff, or coverage necessary for the law to be effective. Legislators frequently find it easier simply to pass a beautifully worded resolution or set up a voluntary commission that has no power.

Approval, Implementation, and Monitoring

1. Once a bill passes both houses, efforts must be directed to getting the governor to sign it into law. Sometimes a governor will sign a bill but later try to cut funding to your new program because of budgetary problems. Also, agencies responsible for implementing a law sometimes perform unsatisfactorily and need to be monitored.

2. A full- or part-time person working in the capitol is invaluable for keeping organizations aware of legislative and executive activities that may affect hearing-impaired people. Those

states that have set up commissions or councils for deaf people have been extremely successful in developing friendly, working relationships with executive staffs and legislators. But it is you, the committed voters, who will make the difference.

3. Use the media. Newspaper and television stories can bring public attention and support to your bill and increase legislative awareness.

4. Work with the National Center for Law and the Deaf (NCLD) on drafting the bill and comparing what other states have done. The NCLD is a free resource to help you at every step of the legislative process.

Working with public officials can be a stimulating, rewarding, yet frustrating experience. They are elected by you and are accountable, finally, to you. So make your views known. Remember Benjamin Franklin's advice: "We must all hang together, or assuredly we shall all hang separately."

State Commissions

Deaf people have worked with state legislatures to see that agencies are established to provide necessary services. The agencies currently in existence take various forms; usually they are constituted as state commissions or councils for deaf people.

At least twenty states now have commissions, councils, or other agencies specifically concerned with providing services to deaf people.* These commissions usually advocate for the needs of deaf citizens by advising the state legislature and by providing liaison with various agencies to secure and coordinate services. Another purpose is to collect and disseminate information about deafness, especially demographic and other data that serve to raise public consciousness about deaf people. Some agencies also coordinate or provide services, including information, referral, individual advocacy, counseling, and interpreters. A goal of some commissions is to create service projects such as job development programs.

The typical commission has from nine to twenty members, including deaf citizens, parents of deaf children, and representatives of various state agencies, professions serving deaf people, and organizations of deaf people.

There are three basic organizational structures for state commissions: Commissions directly funded by the state, those with independent budgets within their agency or department, and those with no separate budget within their agency or department.

Commissions that are independent. They report to the governor and submit their budgets directly to the legislature or governor. Connecticut, Texas, and Virginia have commissions on this model.

Connecticut's commission is a statewide coordinating and advocacy agency

---

*See Appendix E for the titles and addresses of the state commissions or councils that have been established to date.

that provides information, 24-hour-a-day interpreter services in a complete range of settings, interpreter training, counseling, referral, consultation on communication problems in mental health facilities, and representation of deaf citizen interests before public agencies and private industry.

Texas's commission, the first in the nation, was created in 1971 and is responsible for providing all services that are not the responsibility of other state agencies. It serves as an information clearinghouse; provides interpreter services in courts, hospitals, and government offices at no charge; and hires deaf senior citizens to visit other elderly deaf people.

The Virginia Council for the Deaf

coordinates a statewide interpreter service, consults with state agencies and institutions on the unique problems of deafness, evaluates state programs for their relevance and effectiveness, and provides information to the state government on the rights and needs of deaf Virginians. Recognizing that underemployment is a major problem of deaf workers, the commission established an Industrial Relations Committee to identify and suggest ways to meet needs of deaf workers.

Commissions that are independent parts of another agency. They are directly responsible to the head of the umbrella agency. Massachusetts and North Carolina are examples of this kind of commission.

Massachusetts's Office of Deafness is part of the state rehabilitation commission, although not under its jurisdiction. Its director is appointed by the state secretary of human services. The office studies the service needs of deaf people and then advises and recommends priorities to state officials and agencies. It acts as an information clearinghouse and reviews budget requests from state agencies, making comments and recommendations on them. It evaluates and monitors state services for deaf people and suggests necessary changes to improve their quality. And it coordinates interpreter services to deaf people and state programs. The office also monitors all bills in the state legislature which affect deaf people.

Established in 1977, North Carolina's Council for the Hearing Impaired acts as an advocate for deaf people, a bureau of information, and an advisor to the secretary of the state department of human resources. The council plans and implements services for deaf people through community service centers, informs deaf people of their rights and available services, makes referrals, coordinates communication between service agencies and deaf clients, and promotes accessible public community services and the training of interpreters. All of its community service programs are administered by the state Division of Vocational Rehabilitation Services.

Commissions that are part of another state agency. They have no separate budget and operate under the authority of the head of that agency. Minnesota, New Jersey, and Wisconsin have commissions of this type.

In addition to the usual information and advisory functions, the Minnesota Department of Public Welfare has a direct service component for deaf people. The Deaf Services Division works to ensure that all services available to hearing people are also available to deaf people. It negotiates for client's rights and does short-term case management, counseling, and referral. It advises welfare departments and other agencies and programs and, in conjunction with the Division of Vocational Rehabilitation, maintains eight regional service centers, each of which is an entry point for deaf people who need the services. Each center has an advisory committee of eight people appointed by the state commissioner of economic security; four advisors are deaf persons or parents of deaf children and four are representatives of county and regional human service agencies.

A Division of the Deaf within the New Jersey Department of Labor and Industry provides information and referral services, coordinates interpreter services, and provides interpreter training and TDD services for public agencies. It is establishing regional community service centers and works with other state agencies to coordinate services. For example, it has a formal, job-related services agreement with the state division of employment services and the state division of vocational rehabilitation.

Wisconsin's State Service Bureau for the Deaf has a forty-year history. From the beginning, state funds were granted to and administered by a private organization, the Wisconsin Association of the Deaf. In 1979 the service bureau was made into a state agency, the Bureau for the Hearing Impaired, as part of the community services division of the Wisconsin Department of Health and Social Services. The new entity will carry out its advisory and service functions with new authority and a greatly expanded staff.

Specific Needs of Deaf People

In some other states, the commission responsible for deaf concerns also represents other physically and mentally handicapped people. Such commissions may be satisfactory if they have a broad base of support. The advantage gained in not dividing community support on accessibility and discrimination issues may be lost, however, if the commission is not fully aware of the problems of deafness and attentive to the special service needs of deaf people.

When a state legislature establishes a commission, it should specifically address deafness in the enabling legislation.* If the commission is to exist for the entire range of physical and mental disabilities, then all disabled groups should be represented on the commission. The enabling legislation should have a clear and comprehensive definition of eligibility and broad application to the entire range of available programs and settings. The HHS regulations to Section 504 are excellent

models.[3] Once established, the commission should be carefully monitored to make sure that its offices, services, and staff are fully accessible to deaf people. The offices should have TDD-equipped telephones, and commission members, staff, and clients should be provided with interpreters and other necessary accommodations. The interpreters should be qualified and certified.

The histories of existing state commissions indicate that those set up specifically for hearing-impaired citizens do not duplicate services already provided by other departments. The commission is simply a central office with special knowledge of the problems and needs of hearing-impaired people. It provides a center for vital information, consultation, and advocacy. It also raises public awareness about deafness and communication barriers.

The primary need of a council or commission is adequate means to perform its task. Funding must be sufficient and stable so that planning may have a predictable and realistic scope. A full-time, paid staff with wide experience in deafness is vital.

---

*See Appendix F for the (amended) enabling legislation that established Virginia's Council for the Deaf. Note the clear and comprehensive definition of eligibility and the adequate degree of authority given to the agency.

Notes

1. Maryland Code Ann., Art. 59, §70–75 (1980)

2. Adapted from S. DuBow, "Communicating with Your Legislators," *Deaf American* 34(3), pp. 34–35. Used by permission of the publisher.

3. 45 *Code of Federal Regulations* §84.2(j)

Appendices

APPENDIX A

Reference Publications
On Deafness and PL 94-142

The Deaf Child and Regular Education (Mainstreaming)

Birch, J. W. *Hearing-Impaired Children in the Mainstream.* Reston, Va.: Council for Exceptional Children, 1975.

Bishop, M. E., ed. *Mainstreaming: Practical Ideas for Mainstreaming Hearing-Impaired Students.* Washington, D.C.: Alexander Graham Bell Association for the Deaf, 1979.

Brill, R. G. *Mainstreaming the Prelingually Deaf Child.* Washington, D.C.: Gallaudet College Press, 1978.

Garretson, M. "Concept of the Least Restrictive Environment." *Gallaudet Alumni Newsletter* 11(16) Special Issue, June 15, 1977, pp. 10–11.

Jacobs, L. M. *A Deaf Adult Speaks Out.* Washington, D.C.: Gallaudet College Press, 1980.

Jensema, C., and Trybus, R. J. *Who Are the Deaf Children in 'Mainstream' Programs?* Washington, D.C.: Gallaudet College Press, 1977.

Karchmer, M. A., and Trybus, R. J. *Reported Emotional/Behavioral Problems Among Hearing Impaired Children in Special Education Programs; United States, 1972–73.* Washington, D.C.: Gallaudet College, 1975.

Katz, L.; Mathis, S. L.; and Merrill, E. C. *The Deaf Child in the Public Schools: A Handbook for Parents of Deaf Children.* Danville, Ill.: Interstate Printers and Publishers, 1978.

Mindel, E. D., and Vernon, M. *They Grow in Silence.* Silver Spring, Md.: National Association of the Deaf, 1971.

Moores, D. F. *Educating the Deaf: Psychology, Principles and Practices.* Boston: Houghton Mifflin, 1977.

Nix, G. W., ed. *Mainstream Education for Hearing-Impaired Children and Youth.* New York: Grune and Stratton Inc., 1976.

Northcutt, W. H. *The Hearing-Impaired Child in the Classroom: Pre-School, Elementary, and Second Years.* Washington, D.C.: Alexander Graham Bell Association, 1973.

Rosen, R. "Deafness and Implications for Mainstreaming." *Gallaudet Alumni Newsletter* 11(16) Special Issue, June 15, 1977, pp. 11–15.

Spradley, J. P., and Spradley, T. S. *Deaf Like Me.* New York: Random House, 1978.

Vernon, M., and Prickett, H. "Mainstreaming: Issues and a Model Plan." *Audiology and Hearing Education* 2(2), pp. 5–11.

PL 94-142

Alexander Graham Bell Association for the Deaf. *Rights of Hearing-Impaired Children.* Washington, D.C.: Alexander Graham Bell Association for the Deaf, 1977.

Council on Exceptional Children. *Primer on Due Process in Education.* Reston, Va.: Council on Exceptional Children, 1977.

Council on Exceptional Children. *Primer on IEP for Handicapped Children.* Reston, Va.: Council on Exceptional Children, 1977.

DuBow, S. "P.L. 94-142." *American Annals of the Deaf* 122(5), pp. 468–469.

Gallaudet College. *Parents' Guide to Individualized Education Program.* Washington, D.C.: Gallaudet College, 1978.

Kendall Demonstration Elementary School. *Kendall Guide to Assessment: A Handbook for Parents.* Washington, D.C.: Kendall Demonstration Elementary School, Gallaudet College, 1978.

Kendall Demonstration Elementary School. *Kendall School and P.L. 94-142.* Washington, D.C.: Kendall Demonstration Elementary School, Gallaudet College, 1977.

National Committee for Citizens in Education. *Developing Leadership for Parent/Citizen Groups.* Columbia, Md.: National Committee for Citizens in Education, 1976.

APPENDIX B

Appropriate Public Education: Sample Letters of Request

I. Request for Evaluation

> (Your Address)
> (Date)
>
> Superintendent of Schools
> (Local Education Agency)
> (Address)
> (City, State, Zip Code)
>   Re: (Name of Child)   Date of Birth: (Date)
>
> Dear (Sir or Madam):
>   This is to advise you that I have been (retained) (requested) to represent Mr. and Mrs. (name) in connection with their efforts to obtain a free appropriate public education for (child's name). My clients suspect that their (son) (daughter) is (described suspected handicapping condition) and desire an immediate evaluation leading to an individualized education program meeting for placement in a program appropriate for their child's abilities. (Name of child) was born on (month, day, year) and is currently (describe present educational placement).
>   Would you please schedule (child's name) for an evaluation as soon as possible pursuant to Public Law 94-142 and the implementing federal and state regulations. Please advise me when and where Mr. and Mrs. (name) should bring their child for (his) (her) evaluation.
>   Thank you very much. With best wishes, I am,
>
>   Very truly yours,
>
>   (Your name)
>
>   We join in this request for the purpose of consenting to the requested evaluation.
>
>   _____
>   (signature)
>   Mr. (name)
>
> (date)
>
>   _____
>   (signature)
>   Mrs. (name)

Appendix B is adapted from R. Shepard, "The Repudiation of Plato: A Lawyer's Guide to the Educational Rights of Handicapped Children," *University of Richmond Law Review* 13(83) Summer 1979, pp. 842–845. Used by permission of the publisher.

II. Request and Authorization for Records

(Your Address)
(Date)

Superintendent of Schools
(Local Education Agency)
(Address)
(City, State, Zip Code)
    Re: (Name of Child)   Date of Birth: (Date)

Dear (Sir or Madam):

    This is to advise you that I have been (retained) (requested) to represent Mr. and Mrs. (name) in connection with their efforts to obtain a free appropriate public education for (child's name). In connection with this representation I wish to secure copies of all the school records, tests and reports on this child and (will be at your office on (date) at (time) to examine and secure copies of these records) (would like copies of these records sent to me at my office along with any bill for copying as soon as possible).

    These records are sought pursuant to the provisions of Public Law 94-142 and the "Buckley Amendment" and their implementing regulations. Mr. and Mrs. (name) have joined in this letter to authorize release of the records to me. With best wishes, I am,

Very truly yours,

(Your name)

    We, the parents of (child's name) hereby authorize the release of our child's complete school records to (your name) as our (representative) (attorney).

(signature)
_____
Mr. (name)

(date)

(signature)
_____
Mrs. (name)

III. Request for Local Due Process Hearing

(Your Address)
(Date)

Chairman, School Board
(Local Education Agency)
(Address)
(City, State, Zip Code)
    Re: (Name of Child)   Date of Birth: (Date)

Dear (Sir or Madam):

This is to advise you that I have been (retained) (requested) to represent Mr. and Mrs. (name) in connection with their efforts to obtain a free appropriate public education for (child's name). Mr. and Mrs. (name) do not agree with the (evaluation) (placement recommended pursuant to the IEP meeting) of (child's name) and wish to request a hearing on this matter pursuant to Public Law 94-142 and its implementing State and federal Regulations. We would like for this hearing to be scheduled as soon as possible. Please advise me of the name, address and telephone number of the hearing officer as soon as his or her identity is ascertained. I would also request that a verbatim written transcript be prepared of the hearing when held.

Please notify Mr. and Mrs. (name) and me of the time, date and place for the hearing when it is scheduled, and it might be (desirable) to check with me regarding the proposed date prior to sending out any notices so as to avoid a conflict that would require rescheduling the hearing. Mr. and Mrs. (name) have joined in this letter to confirm their request for a hearing. Thank you very much. With best wishes, I am,

Very truly yours,

(Your name)

We, the parents of (child's name) join in and affirm this request for a hearing regarding our child's education.

_____
(signature)
Mr. (name)

(date)

_____
(signature)
Mrs. (name)

IV. Request for State Review

(Your address)
(Date)

(Superintendent of Public Instruction)
(State Department of Education)
(Address)
(City, State, Zip Code)
    Re: (Name of Child)   Date of Birth: (Date)
        (Locality)

Dear (Sir or Madam):

This is to advise you that I have been (retained) (requested) to represent Mr. and Mrs. (name) in connection with their efforts to obtain a free appropriate public education for (child's name) in the (local school division) schools. Mr. and Mrs. (name) do not agree with the decision reached on (date) by (name of local hearing officer), the hearing officer for the (local school division) and desire a review of (his) (her) decision pursuant to Public Law 94-142 and its implementing State and federal Regulations. We would like for this review hearing to be scheduled as soon as possible as we request the opportunity to present both written and oral arguments to the hearing officer. Please advise me of the name, address, and telephone number of the hearing officer assigned as soon as his or her identity is ascertained.

Please notify Mr. and Mrs. (name) and me of the time, date and place for the hearing when it is scheduled, and it might be desirable to check with me regarding the proposed date prior to sending out any notices so as to avoid a conflict that would require rescheduling the hearing. Mr. and Mrs. (name) have joined in this letter to confirm their request for a review hearing. Thank you very much. With best wishes, I am,

Very truly yours,

(Your name)

We, the parents of (child's name) join in and affirm this request for a review of the local hearing officer's decision of (date) in (local school division) regarding our child's education.

(signature)
_____
Mr. (name)

(date)

(signature)
_____
Mrs. (name)

APPENDIX C

Providing Interpreter Service: One Agency Example

Memorandum

DATE: Nov. 15, 1979

TO: All Associate Commissioners
All Acting Associate Commissioners
All Regional Commissioners
All Assistant Regional Commissioners, Field Operations
All Area Directors
All DO's/BO's/TSC's

FROM: Acting Director for Civil Rights and Equal Opportunity
Social Security Administration
Department of Health, Education, and Welfare

SUBJECT: Providing Interpreter Service for the Hearing-Impaired in Social Security Administration Proceedings—ACTION

Pursuant to Section 504 of the Rehabilitation Act of 1973 as amended, SSA has an obligation to make sure that all programs and facilities are accessible to handicapped persons. This includes making certain that there is accurate communication with the hearing-impaired.

In October of 1978 the Associate Commissioner for Program Operations issued a see below [sic] outlining the circumstances under which SSA could purchase interpreter service. However, some organizations of the hearing-impaired have now requested more specific guidelines. In addition, we have had many recent contacts indicating that there is some confusion as to how our policy is to be implemented, and that some district and branch office employees are unaware that interpreters can be hired by SSA.

Accordingly, this memorandum will outline in greater detail the procedures to be followed. A Claims Manual section will be issued on this subject in the near future.

Provision of Interpreters

It is the policy of the Social Security Administration to insure maximum accessibility of social security programs to the hearing-impaired in all agency proceedings concerning application for, or receipt, suspension, revocation, underpayment or overpayment of benefits under the Social Security Act. At times, this will include the local purchase of interpreter services for the hearing-impaired. This procedure is authorized within the local purchase authority delegated to district and branch office managers when it is necessary for effective communication. The claimant shall be informed immediately by the appropriate district or branch office employee that he or she has the right to interpreter service in accordance with the options listed below, and may request an interpreter at the agency's expense at any stage of agency proceedings, if he or she feels that effective communication is not occurring.

Several options for the provision of interpreter service exist:

1. The hearing-impaired person may provide his or her own interpreter at no cost to SSA;

2. A district or branch office may use its own employee who is proficient in sign language, or may borrow a qualified SSA employee from another office;

3. A qualified interpreter may be borrowed from another HEW component or from another Federal agency;

4. Free community service may be secured; or

5. SSA may purchase the needed service.

Note: An SSA or other Federal employee is considered to be qualified to sign if he or she is able accurately and simultaneously to *express* (send signs to the hearing-impaired person) and *receive* (understand signs from a hearing-impaired person) in sign language.

Conditions for Purchase of Interpreter Services

Initial Claims Proceedings

The above discussion will help to determine when the purchase of interpreter services is needed. The purchase of the services of an interpreter may be made when the following conditions are met:

1. There are no available SSA or other Federal employees who are able to communicate effectively with the hearing-impaired claimant.

   Normally, effective communication will require the use of an employee who is able to sign rather than written communication. If either the employee-interpreter or hearing-impaired claimant indicates he or she has difficulty communicating, then a non-SSA interpreter shall be obtained. In no event shall a hearing-impaired person be required to use an interpreter with whom he or she is unable to communicate.

2. There are no available community organizations which offer free interpreter services for the hearing-impaired.

   The district or branch office management shall initially survey the appropriate local agencies to determine the availability of free services. If free community services are available, the district or branch offices shall maintain a listing of available resources containing information such as the number of available interpreters and the timeliness with which a volunteer would be available in the office to interpret an interview. It shall be the primary responsibility of the office employee to secure the free outside service if the hearing-impaired individual has none of his or her own.

   If community services are not available or become unavailable, there shall be periodic checks (about every six months) to see if free interpreter services are available. These periodic checks should be part of the normal community relations activities of the district or branch office.

3. Approval for the purchase of service has been secured in advance.

Purchase may be made via issuance of SF-147 or the use of imprest funds in accordance with ADS Guide OPO F:130–34, Small Purchase Procedures. Both require approval before a service can be utilized.

When an office is notified that a hearing-impaired person wishes to come in for an interview and does not have his or her own interpreter, a determination must be made as to the availability of free community service. If none is available, and if no SSA or other Federal employee is available, the appropriate district or branch office employee shall make arrangements for the purchase of service, shall secure the necessary approval described herein, and shall notify the hearing-impaired individual and the interpreter as to the time and place of the interview. Every effort shall be made to conduct the interview as quickly as possible.

If a hearing-impaired person comes to an office with an interpreter without prior arrangement for the interview, and if the hearing-impaired person requests SSA to pay for the interpreter's service, every effort shall be made to secure approval of the purchase immediately so that the interview can be conducted while the hearing-impaired person is in the office (naturally the other criteria must also be met).

4. A "qualified interpreter" is available.

An interpreter shall be deemed qualified if he or she is certified by the National Registry of Interpreters or by a state registry of interpreters, or if he or she is on a list of qualified interpreters compiled by the National Association of the Deaf or any state association of the deaf.

It is recognized that qualified interpreters are not available everywhere in the country. In the event that a qualified interpreter as described above is unavailable, the agency shall provide an interpreter who is acceptable to both the hearing-impaired person and the agency.

Appeal Proceedings

A hearing-impaired individual has the right to have an interpreter available at all stages of the appeals procedure. If the hearing-impaired individual does not have his or her own interpreter, SSA shall purchase such service in accordance with the conditions outlined above.

Interpreters—Appointment; Compensation

District and branch office employees shall assist the claimant in locating an interpreter and arrange for the purchase of an interpreter whenever this is requested by the claimant.

Any interpreter, other than a Federal employee, appointed under this policy shall be paid a reasonable fee by the agency for his or her services. The fees should be based on prevailing rates and should reflect input from associations for the deaf or hearing-impaired.

SSA Notification to the Hearing-Impaired Community Concerning the Availability of Interpreter Service

In order to ensure maximum accessibiity to all SSA programs by the hearing-impaired, district and branch offices shall take all possible steps to notify hearing-impaired persons of the policies contained herein. Wherever possible, public service announcements shall be made through the news media on an ongoing basis. In addition, district and branch office personnel shall provide the information contained herein to local organizations of the hearing-impaired, community service organizations, or social service agencies as part of their ongoing community relations effort.

Each district and branch office shall maintain a notice to the public on its bulletin boards containing the policies outlined herein.

Note: In making arrangements for an interpreter where the interview is in connection with filing a claim, care must be taken to insure that there is no loss of benefits because an application is not filed timely.

(Signed)

Peter F. Velasquez

APPENDIX D

A Model Act to Provide for the Appointment of Interpreters For Hearing-Impaired Individuals For Administrative, Legislative, And Judicial Proceedings

I. Public Policy

It is the policy of this state to secure the rights of hearing-impaired persons who, because of impaired hearing, cannot readily understand or communicate in spoken language and who consequently cannot equally participate in or benefit from proceedings, programs, and activities of the courts, legislative bodies, administrative agencies, licensing commission, departments, and boards of the state and its subdivisions unless qualified interpreters are available to assist them.

II. Definitions

As used in this chapter, the following terms have the following meanings:

1. "Appointing authority" means the presiding officer or similar official in any court, board, commission, authority, department, agency, or legislative body, or in any proceeding of any nature where a qualified interpreter is required pursuant to this Act.
2. A "hearing-impaired person" means a person who, because of a hearing impairment, has difficulty understanding oral communication.
3. "Qualified interpreter" means a sign language or oral interpreter as provided in Sections IV and VII of this Act.
4. "Intermediary interpreter" means any hearing-impaired person who is able to assist in providing an accurate interpretation between spoken English and sign language, or between variants of sign language, by acting as an intermediary interpreter.

III. Interpreter Required in the Following Situations

1. Whenever a hearing-impaired person is a party or witness at any stage of any judicial or quasi-judicial proceeding in this state or in its political subdivisions—including but not limited to civil and criminal court proceedings, grand jury proceedings, proceedings before a magistrate, juvenile proceedings, adoption proceedings, mental health commitment proceedings, and any proceeding in which a hearing-impaired person may be subjected to confinement or criminal sanction—the appointing authority shall appoint and pay for a qualified interpreter to interpret the proceedings to the hearing-impaired person and to interpret the hearing-impaired person's testimony.

2. Whenever a juvenile whose parent or parents are hearing-impaired is brought before a court for any reason whatsoever, the court shall appoint and pay for a qualified interpreter to interpret the proceedings to the hearing-impaired parent and to interpret the hearing-impaired parent's testimony.

3. In any hearing, proceeding, or other program or activity of any department, board, licensing authority, commission, or administrative agency of the state or of its political subdivisions, the appointing authority shall appoint and pay for a qualified interpreter for the hearing-impaired participants.

4. Whenever a hearing-impaired person is a witness before any legislative committee or subcommittee, or legislative research or study committee or subcommittee or commission authorized by the state legislature or legislative body of any political subdivision of the state, the appointing authority shall appoint and pay for a qualified interpreter to interpret the proceedings to the hearing-impaired person and to interpret the hearing-impaired person's testimony.

5. Whenever a hearing-impaired person is arrested for an alleged violation of a criminal law, including a local ordinance, the arresting officer shall procure a qualified interpreter for any interrogation, warning, notification of

rights, or taking of a statement. No hearing-impaired arrestee otherwise eligible for release shall be held in custody pending arrival of an interpreter. No answer, statement, or admission, written or oral, made by a hearing-impaired person in reply to a question of a law enforcement officer or any other person having a prosecutorial function in any criminal or quasi-criminal proceeding may be used against that hearing-impaired person unless either the statement was made or elicited through a qualified interpreter and was made knowingly, voluntarily, and intelligently or, in the case of waiver, unless the court makes a special finding that the statement made by the hearing-impaired person was made knowingly, voluntarily, and intelligently.

6. Where it is the policy and practice of a court of this state or of its political subdivision to appoint counsel for indigent people, the appointing authority shall appoint and pay for a qualified interpreter for hearing-impaired indigent people to assist in communication with counsel in all phases of the preparation and presentation of the case.

IV. Preliminary Determination of Interpreter's Qualifications

Before appointing an interpreter, the appointing authority shall make a preliminary determination, on the basis of the hearing-impaired person's testimony, that the interpreter is able to accurately communicate with and translate information to and from the hearing-impaired person involved. If the interpreter is not able to provide effective communication with the hearing-impaired person, the appointing authority shall appoint another qualified interpreter.

V. Intermediary Interpreter to Be Used

If a qualified interpreter is unable to render a satisfactory interpretation without the aid of an intermediary interpreter, the appointing authority shall appoint an intermediary interpreter to assist the qualified interpreter, subject to the same provisions that govern a qualified interpreter under this Act.

VI. Interpreter in Full View

Whenever an interpreter is required to be appointed under

this Act, the appointing authority may not commence proceedings until the appointed interpreter is in full view of and spatially situated to assure effective communication with the hearing-impaired participants.

VII. *Coordination of Interpreter Requests*

1. [The Department of Human Resources] shall establish, maintain, update, and distribute a list of qualified interpreters. The Department shall obtain the names of interpreters for this list from the state association of the deaf, state registry of interpreters for the deaf, and state schools for the deaf.

2. Whenever an interpreter is required under this Act, the appointing authority shall use one of the interpreters on the [Department of Human Resources] list. If none of the listed interpreters is available or if an interpreter is unable to provide effective communication with the particular hearing-impaired person, then the appointing authority shall appoint any other person who is able to accurately and simultaneously communicate with and translate information to and from the particular hearing-impaired person involved.

VIII. *Oath of Interpreter*

Before he or she begins to interpret, each interpreter appointed under this Act shall take an oath that he or she will make a true interpretation in an understandable manner to and for the person for whom he or she is appointed to the best of his or her skills and judgment.

IX. *Compensation*

An interpreter appointed under this Act is entitled to a reasonable fee for his or her services, including waiting time, reimbursement for necessary travel, and subsistence expenses. The fee shall be based on any fee schedule for interpreters recommended by the [Department of Human Resources] or prevailing market rates. Reimbursement for necessary travel and subsistence expenses shall be at rates provided by law for state employees generally.

X. Waiver

The right of a hearing-impaired person to an interpreter may not be waived except by a hearing-impaired person who requests a waiver in writing. Such waiver is subject to the approval of counsel to the hearing-impaired person, if existent, and is subject to the approval of the appointing authority. In no event is the failure of the hearing-impaired person to request an interpreter deemed a waiver of that right.

XI. Privileged Communications

Whenever a hearing-impaired person communicates through an interpreter to any person under such circumstances that the communication would be privileged and said person could not be compelled to testify as to the communications, said privilege shall apply to the interpreter as well.

XII. Visual Recording

The appointing authority, on his or her own motion or on the motion of a party to the proceedings, may order that the testimony of the hearing-impaired person and the interpretation thereof be electronically recorded (visually) for use in verification of the official transcript of the proceedings.

APPENDIX E

States That Have Established Commissions Or Councils Concerned with Deaf People

Arizona: Arizona Council for the Deaf
1400 W. Washington St., Room 124
Phoenix, AZ 85007
(602) 255-3323

Arkansas: Office of the Deaf and
   Hearing Impaired
Rehabilitation Services
P.O. Box 3781
Little Rock, AR 72203
(501) 371-2502

California: Social Services for the Deaf
744 P St.
Sacramento, CA 95814
(916) 486-8570

Connecticut: Connecticut Commission
   on the Deaf and Hearing Impaired
40 Woodland St.
Hartford, CT 06105
(203) 566-7414 (Voice/TTY)

Georgia: Council on the Deaf
c/o Division of Rehabilitation Services
47 Trinity Ave. SW
Atlanta, GA 30334
(404) 656-2913 (Voice/TTY)

Iowa: Deaf Services of Iowa
Iowa State Department of Health
Lucas State Office Building
Des Moines, IA 50319
(515) 281-3164 (Voice/TTY)

Louisiana: Louisiana Commission for
   the Deaf
P.O. Box 44371
Baton Rouge, LA 70804
(504) 342-2287

Maryland: Commission for the Hearing
   Impaired
897 Windsong Dr.
Arnold, MD 21012

Massachusetts: Massachusetts Office of
   Deafness
20 Park Plaza
Boston, MA 02116
(617) 727-5106/5236 (Voice/TTY)

Michigan: Division of Deaf and
   Deafened
Michigan Department of Labor
309 N. Washington Square
Box 30015
Lansing, MI 48909
(517) 373-0378 (Voice/TTY)

Minnesota: Deaf Services Division
Department of Public Welfare
658 Cedar Ave.
St. Paul, MN 55155
(612) 296-3980/4850 (Voice/TTY)

Nebraska: Commission for the Hearing
   Impaired
4600 Valley Rd.
Lincoln, NB 68510
(402) 471-3593 (Voice/TTY)

New Jersey: Division of the Deaf
Department of Labor and Industry
114 W. State St.
Trenton, NJ 08625
(609) 984-7281 (Voice/TTY)

North Carolina: North Carolina Council
for the Hearing Impaired
Division of Vocational Rehabilitation
Services
620 N. West St.
P.O. Box 26053
Raleigh, NC 27611
(919) 733-5920 (Voice/TTY)

Oklahoma: Oklahoma Commission on
the Deaf and Hearing Impaired
4901 Lincoln
P.O. Box 25352
Oklahoma City, OK 73125
(405) 521-2754 (Voice/TTY)

South Dakota: Communication Services
for the Deaf
421 N. Lewis
Sioux Falls, SD 57103
(605) 339-6718 (Voice/TTY)

Tennessee: Tennessee Council for the
Hearing Impaired
1808 West End Building
Nashville, TN 37203
(615) 741-2521 (Voice/TTY)

Texas: Texas Commission for the Deaf
P.O. Box 12904, Capitol Station
Austin, TX 78711
(512) 475-2493 (Voice/TTY)

Virginia: Virginia Council for the Deaf
801 E. Broad St.
Richmond, VA 23219
(804) 786-1381

Wisconsin: Bureau for the Hearing
Impaired
Department of Health and Social
Services
P.O. Box 7851
Madison, WI 53707
(608) 266-8081/8083 (Voice/TTY)

APPENDIX F

Enabling Legislation for a State Commission: The Example of Virginia

Virginia Council for the Deaf

Va. Code §63.1-85.1.   Council established; appointment, terms and qualifications of members; meetings; chairman.

       §63.1-85.2.   Director.

       §63.1-85.3.   Deaf persons defined and classified.

       §63.1-85.4.   Powers and duties of Council.

       §63.1-85.4:1 Statewide interpreter service.

       §63.1-85.5.   Register of the deaf to be maintained by Department of Health; further duties of Department.

       §63.1-85.6.   [Repealed.]

       §63.1-85.7.   Gifts and donations; disposition of moneys received.

§63.1-85.1. Council established; appointment, terms and qualifications of members; meetings; chairman. —(a) There is hereby established a Virginia Council for the Deaf, hereinafter in this chapter referred to as the Council.

(b) The Council shall be composed of fourteen members from the Department of Health; one member from the Department of Education; one member from the Department of Mental Hygiene and Hospitals; one member from the Department of Vocational Rehabilitation; one member from the Department of Welfare; one member from the Virginia School for the Deaf and Blind at Staunton; one member from the Virginia School at Hampton; and seven other members, one of whom shall be an audiologist, and one of whom shall be an otolaryngologist, and of the remaining five members at least two shall be persons who are deaf and the remaining three shall be representatives of professions, community agencies or organizations concerned with the health, education, rehabilitation and welfare of the deaf. No person shall be eligible to serve more than two successive terms (other than the representatives of the above named State agencies and institutions), except that a person appointed to fill a vacancy may serve two additional successive terms. The Council shall meet at the call of the chairman, who shall be selected by the Council from among its membership, but no less than four times a year. (1972, c. 543; 1974, cc. 44, 45.)

§63.1-85.2. Director. —The director may be either a deaf person or one with normal hearing, but shall be a trained professional who is experienced in problems of the deaf and skilled in the use of manual communication, commonly referred to as sign language. (1972, c. 543; 1978, c. 603.)

§63.1-85.3. Deaf persons defined and classified. —For the purposes of this chapter, deaf persons are defined as those in whom the sense of hearing is nonfunctional for the ordinary purposes of life, including two distinct classes based on the time of the loss of hearing: (1) the congenital deaf—those who were born deaf; and (2) the adventitiously deaf—those who were born with normal hearing but in whom the sense of hearing becomes nonfunctional later through illness or accident. (1972, c. 543.)

§63.1-85.4. Powers and duties of Council. —The Council shall act as a bureau of information to the deaf, to State agencies and institutions providing services for the deaf, local agencies of government, and other public or private community agencies and programs. In this respect the Council shall:

(a) Inform the deaf of the availability of the provisions of the Virginia Council for the Deaf and such other services available for the deaf at all levels of government;

(b) Establish a framework for consultation and cooperation among the State agencies and institutions represented on the Council;

(c) Advise the several agencies and institutions represented on the Council concerning the administration of, preparation of regulations for and operation of their programs;

(d) Continuously study the handicapping problems of deaf of all ages, review the administration and operation of the various programs for deaf in the Commonwealth and make recommendations with respect thereto to the several agencies and institutions represented on the Council as the Council deems necessary and proper;

(e) Make and submit to the Governor and the General Assembly annual reports of its finding and recommendations;

(f) Conduct independent evaluations of programs for the deaf in the Commonwealth and publish and distribute the results thereof;

(g) The Council may obtain the services of such professional, technical and clerical personnel as may be necessary to enable them to carry out its function under this section and to contract for such services as may be necessary to carry out its evaluation functions;

(h) The Council shall cooperate with the schools for the deaf as provided for in chapter 19 (§23-254 et seq.) of Title 23 of the Code insofar as may be practicable. (1972, c. 543; 1977, c. 668.)

§63.1-85.4:1. Statewide interpreter service. —The Council is authorized to establish, maintain and coordinate a Statewide service to provide courts, State and local legislative bodies and agencies, both public and private, and deaf persons who request the same with qualified interpreters for the deaf out of such funds as may be appropriated to the Council for these purposes. Those courts and State and local agencies which have funds designated to employ qualified interpreters shall pay for the actual cost of such interpreters. The Council is further authorized to establish and maintain lists of qualified interpreters for the deaf to be available to the courts, State and local legislative bodies and agencies, both public and private, and to deaf persons. (1978, c. 603.)

§63.1-85.5. Register of the deaf to be maintained by Department of Health; further duties of Department. —(a) The Department of Health shall prepare and maintain a complete register of the deaf in the State which shall describe the condition, cause of deafness and such other facts as may be of value. Each physician or other person who, upon examination of the hearing of any person, determines that such person is a deaf person shall immediately report the name and address of such person to the Department of Health.

(b) The Department of Health shall make inquiries concerning the cause of deafness, ascertain what portion of such cases are preventable and adopt and enforce proper preventive measures.

(c) The Department of Health shall make information contained on the register available to the several agencies and institutions directly connected with the administration of programs providing services to the deaf; or for research purposes may make the information available to an organization or individual engaged in research only for purposes directly connected with the administration of programs relating to the deaf, including research for the development of new knowledge or techniques, which would be useful in the administration of the program, but only if the organization or individual furnishes satisfactory assurance that the information will be used solely for the purposes for which it is provided; that it shall not be released to persons not connected with the study; and that the final product of the research will not reveal any information that may serve to identify any person about whom the information has been obtained without the written consent of such person and the Department of Health. (1972, c. 543.)

§63.1-85.6. Repealed by Acts 1980, c. 728.

(Cross reference.—For present provisions as to compensation of members of boards, commissions, committees, councils and similar bodies, see §2.1-20.2 et seq.)

§63.1-85.7. Gifts and donations; disposition of moneys received. —The Council is authorized to receive such gifts and donations, either from public or private sources, as may be offered unconditionally or under such conditions as in the judgment of the Council are proper and consistent with this chapter. All moneys received as gifts or donations or State appropriations shall be deposited in the State treasury to be used by the Council to defray expenses in performing its duties. A full report of all gifts and donations accepted, together with the names of the donors and the respective amounts contributed by each, and all disbursements therefrom, shall be submitted annually to the Governor by the Council. (1972, c. 543.)

Index

Georgia: Council on the Deaf, 182; mental health law, 83
Gottfried, Sue, 136
Grievance procedures. See Complaint procedures

H

Habeas corpus, 78, 79
Halderman. See Pennhurst v. Halderman
Handicapped: definition of, 15–16; special treatment of the, HEW regulations, 17; equal opportunity for the, HEW regulations, 16–17
Handicapped children, education, 27–40; statistics, 27
Handicapped postsecondary students: college admission, 43, 44; rights of, 44–49
Hard of hearing, definition under PL 94-142, 28
Health, Education, and Welfare, U.S. Department of. See Health and Human Services/Health, Education, and Welfare, U.S. Department of
Health and Human Services/Health, Education, and Welfare, U.S. Department of, 12, 15, 16, 17, 18, 19, 20, 22, 24, 49, 50, 60, 61, 85, 112, 114, 134
Health services: and Section 504, 55–56; right to medical and psychiatric treatment, 81; staff training, 69–70. See also Emergency care; Hospitals; Mental health services
Hearing aids, 69, 82; background noise, 6, 33, 64, 93; telephone switch, 8, 148–149
Hendrick Hudson School District v. Rowley, 33
Hospitals, 58–69; auxiliary aids, provision of, 60, 61, 63–64; consent forms, 64; guidelines for communication with the hearing impaired, 68–69; guidelines for service, 64–67; intercoms, 63–64, 69; interpreters, 60, 67, 68; orientation, 64; Section 504 compliance, 63; staff awareness, 64, 68–69. See also Emergency care; Health services
Hughes, Harry (Maryland governor), 152

I

IEP. See Individualized Education Program
Illinois, 154; Division of Rehabilitation Services, 47; Institute of Technology, 47; Mental Health Code, 83
Incompetency: and criminal proceedings, 76; and mental health programs, 76
Individualized Education Program (IEP), 29–39; aids and services for deaf children, 33; appeals, 39; contents, 30–31; definition, 29–30; due process hearing, 37–39; manual language components, 35; parents'

role in developing, 30, 31–33; procedural safeguards, 37–39; sample request letters, 166–169; specifying teaching method, 34–35; supplementary services, 33
Information services for the hearing impaired, 19–20, 64
Interior, U.S. Department of the, 112
International Association of Parents of the Deaf, 36
Interpreter referral centers, 107
Interpreters: appointment procedure, 57; attorney-client privilege, 127; certification, 2, 107; competence, 2, 57, 124; definition of, 2; for deaf-blind, 2; guidelines for use of, 3; inexperienced, 2, 4; lighting for, 19; oral, 2; payment of, 45, 46, 49, 118, 119; qualifications, 123; required skills, 2–4; training, 107
Interpreters, provision of: civil and administrative proceedings, 126–127; colleges and universities, 45; comprehensive rehabilitation centers, 107; court proceedings, 118–119; deaf parents, 30, 37, 40; deaf students, 46–51; deaf workers, 91, 92, 95; federal and state courts, 117–118; federal government employment, 99; food stamp offices, 56; hospitals, 60, 63, 64–67; job training programs, 96; legal proceedings, 117; meetings, 19; model act, 176–180; oral examinations, 44; pre-trial, 125; prison, 126; Social Security Administration, 57, 170–174; social service agencies, 55, 57; victims and complainants, 123; when arrested, 119–124
Iowa, Deaf Services of, 182

J

Jackson, Theon, 75–77
Job training programs, 96
Justice, U.S. Department of, 12, 20, 52, 119, 123, 124, 125, 126, 128

K

KCET-TV, 136
Kean College, 46
Kentucky, 127

L

Labor, U.S. Department of, 105
Lang, Donald, 74–75, 76, 77
Law enforcement agencies, provision of interpreters, 123

Stickney. *See* Wyatt v. Stickney

Supreme Court, U.S.: case of Theon Jackson, 75–77; due process rights, 126; Hendrick Hudson School District v. Rowley, 33; Miranda v. Arizona, 119; O'Connor v. Donaldson, 78; Pennhurst v. Halderman, 82; television, 135–136; Southeastern Community College v. Davis, 44, 49–52

Sussman, Allen, 151–152

T

TDD. *See* Telecommunication Device for the Deaf

Teachers, trained, 36–37

Teaching methods, 34–35

TeleCaption units, 134

Telecommunication Device for the Deaf, 7–8, 18, 20, 139; basic service, 148; certification of the hearing impaired, 141; for health care providers, 62; in employment, 92–93; in hospitals, 58, 63, 64, 67; long-distance rate reduction, 141–142; new technology, 147–148; obsolete equipment, 148; operator, 144; police departments, 127; post offices, 122–123; public telephones, 145; rental, 147; telephone directory listing, 7–8; toll-free number, 144

Telephone, 7–8, 139–143; amplifier switches, 8; auditory alarm systems, 19; customer services, 143–144; federal and state regulation, 140; public, 112; special equipment, 145–146; use with hearing aids, 8, 148–149; use in job, 90

Television, 131, 133–137; emergency bulletins, 131, 133; FCC requirements, 134–136; public service announcements, 20. *See also* Captioning

Tennessee, 127; Council for the Hearing Impaired, 183

Texas, state commission for the deaf, 159, 183

Texas, University of. *See* Camenisch v. University of Texas

"Total communication," definition of, 34–35

Transportation, U.S. Department of, 112

Treasury, U.S. Department of. *See* Office of Revenue Sharing

Trial records, 52

Trials, preparation for, interpreters, 125

TTY (Teletypewriter). *See* Telecommunication Device for the Deaf

U

U.S. Constitution, sixth amendment, 124

U.S. government. *See departments by name, e.g., Justice, U.S. Department of, and specific offices and bureaus*

Universities. *See* Colleges and universities

V

Vernon, McCay, 74

Virginia, 58, 127, 154; Council for the Deaf, 58, 159, 183, 184–187

Vocational rehabilitation: agencies, 47–49; counselors, 100; services, 106–107

W

Weinberger. *See* Dixon v. Weinberger

WGBH (TV), 133

Willowbrook State School (New York), 80

Wisconsin: Association of the Deaf, 160; Bureau for the Hearing Impaired, 160, 183; State Service Bureau for the Deaf, 160

Wouri v. Zitnay. *See* Maine, right to habilitation

Wyatt v. Aderholt, 79–80

Wyatt v. Stickney, 79–80